二十世紀最偉大的奇迹之一：人们可以用自己的双手，救活部分突然猝死的病人。

王一鏜

二〇一八年四月

# 心肺脑复苏术操作训练规范

（第二版）

王一镗　陈　彦　编著

上海科学技术出版社

图片在版编目(CIP)数据

心肺脑复苏术操作训练规范/王一镗，陈彦编著.—2版.—上海：上海科学技术出版社，2019.1

ISBN 978-7-5478-4202-7

Ⅰ.①心… Ⅱ.①王…②陈… Ⅲ.①心肺复苏术-技术操作规程 Ⅳ.①R605.974-65

中国版本图书馆CIP数据核字（2018）第220485号

心肺脑复苏术操作训练规范（第二版）

王一镗 陈 彦 编著

上海世纪出版(集团)有限公司<br>上 海 科 学 技 术 出 版 社 出版、发行

(上海钦州南路71号 邮政编码200235 www.sstp.cn)

上海书刊印刷有限公司印刷

开本 787×1092 1/32 印张：1.5

字数：18千字

2007年5月第1版

2019年1月第2版 2019年1月第3次印刷

ISBN 978-7-5478-4202-7/R·1725

定价：10.00元

# 内容提要

近年来，随着猝死、突发疾病、重大事故等新闻报道的增多，人们对心肺复苏这项急救技术已不再陌生，许多城市已在火车站、机场、地铁站等人流密集场所放置了体外自动除颤器（AED）。如何在紧急时刻正确、有效地为伤病人员实施心肺复苏？如何正确使用公共AED进行及时、正确的现场救护？

为大力开展群众性心肺复苏训练，在群众中普及现场急救知识与技术，以组建医疗专业人员与群众救护相结合的急救网络，中国心肺复苏第一人——王一镗教授携陈彦教授以2007年出版的《心肺脑复苏术操作训练规范》为基础，结合2015版美国心脏协会（AHA）心肺复苏指南及其2017年的更新内容，修订出版了这本《心肺脑复苏术操作训练规范》（第二版），重点在于现场心肺复苏操作技术，供各地在开展心肺复苏普及训练时使用。

# 前　言

现代心肺复苏术起源于20世纪五六十年代，并于1974年由美国心脏协会（American Heart Association, AHA）制定了第一个心肺复苏指南。近年来，在世界上一些科技发达国家，急诊医学发展迅速，现场心肺复苏的抢救已标准化、规范化，并加强了对普通公众的急救技能的培训和普及。2015年数据显示，美国公民有50%以上接受过心肺复苏术相关急救培训，旁观者实施心肺复苏术的比例高达46.1%，因而及时挽救了许多伤病人员的生命。

在我国，伴随着社会经济的发展和生活水平的提高，公民的健康素养已有所提升，但心肺复苏术等急救技术的培训和普及率仍较低。以北京和上海等一线城市为例，公众接受心肺复苏术培训的比例也只有10%～15%。因此，在意外伤害和急性病症发生时，往往因事故现场缺少懂得急救的人员，致使伤病员得不到及时、正确的现场救护，因而延误了宝贵的抢救时间，增加了伤病员的痛苦，甚至造成本可以避免的伤残或死亡。

鉴于上述状况，为尽快达到世界急诊医学

的先进水平，亟需大力开展群众性的心肺复苏术培训，在群众中普及现场急救知识与技术，组建医疗专业人员与群众救护相结合的急救网络。美国心脏协会（AHA）心肺复苏指南2015版已发布，并且在2017年做了更新，心肺复苏技术和理念发生了较大转变。为此，编者结合新指南的精神，修订出版了这本《心肺脑复苏术操作训练规范》（第二版），重点在现场心肺复苏，供各地在开展心肺复苏普及训练时使用。

国际人道医学学会 理事
中华医学会灾难医学学会 名誉主任委员
南京医科大学第一附属医院 终身教授
王一镗

2018年5月20日

# 目　　录

第一章

# 心肺脑复苏的意义及主要内容

心跳呼吸骤停和意识丧失，无论在院外还是在院内，都是最紧急的危险情况，心肺复苏术 (cardiopulmonary resuscitation , CPR) 就是对此种危急状况所采用的急救措施。心搏骤停后，20% 以上的幸存者有严重的神经系统后遗症，因此心肺复苏术的成功不仅要求心跳和呼吸的恢复，还必须达到脑功能的恢复，包括智能和工作能力，临床上称之为心搏骤停恢复自主循环后治疗，故 CPR 的全程称之为心肺脑复苏 (cardiopulmonary cerebral resuscitation , CPCR)。

## 一、时间就是生命

据统计，全球每年因心血管疾病死亡人数至少 1.35 亿，我国每年因心跳呼吸骤停而猝死的人数约为 54.4 万，其中 70% ~ 80% 发生在家庭、街道和公共场所中。我国心跳呼吸骤停的急救成功率不到 1%，而且接受过 CPR 培训的公众也只占 9% 左右。但在瑞典等发达国家，心肺复苏急救普及率却达 30%，在美国部分地区甚至高达 50%。对比发现，我国的心肺复苏术普及现状与发达国家差距非常显著。

心跳呼吸突然停止后，循环终止。由于脑细胞对缺氧十分敏感，心搏骤停 10 秒后出现意识丧失，突然倒地，30 秒后出现全身抽搐，1 分钟出现自主呼吸逐渐停止，3 分钟开始出现脑水肿，4 ~ 6 分钟后脑细胞即发生不可逆的死亡。因此，必须争分夺秒，积极抢救。

要使病人得救、避免脑细胞死亡，以便心跳呼吸恢复后意识也能恢复，抢救人员必须在病人心跳停止后立即进行有效的心肺复苏。复苏开始越早，存活率越高。大量实践表明，4 分钟内开始复苏，可能有一半的人被救活；4 ~ 6 分钟开始进行复苏，10% 的人可能被救活；超过 6 分钟开始复苏，存活率仅 4%；10 分钟以上开始复苏，存活率已不足 0.1%。引起心搏骤停的原因甚多，最常见的原因是冠心病，占心源性猝死原因的 80%。

院外心搏骤停死亡率高的原因有以下几方

面。

1. 病人本身耽误了时间（如不了解医学急救常识）；

2. 周围的人（包括家属）不懂急救方法；

3. 在呼叫救护车、等待救护人员到达过程中耽搁了时间；

4. 病人或周围的人做了错误的急救处理。

总之，如周围的人或家属能学会正确的抢救方法，则可避免耽误宝贵的抢救时间。猝死大多是一时性严重心律失常，并非病变已发展到了无法救治的程度。只要抢救及时、正确、有效，许多病人是可望救活的。如广大群众掌握了正确的 CPR 技术，一旦有人心跳突然停止，就能立即得到正确的急救复苏。关键在于要有更多的人学会正确的心肺复苏术，分秒必争地投入抢救，时间就是生命！

## 二、院外心搏骤停的生存链

院外心搏骤停病人的完整生存链包含以下五个环节（图 1），前三项由现场目击者完成。大多数院外心搏骤停是由潜在的心脏问题引起而突发，在最初的几分钟内，由非专业施救者尽早进行心肺复苏和快速除颤是至关重要的。

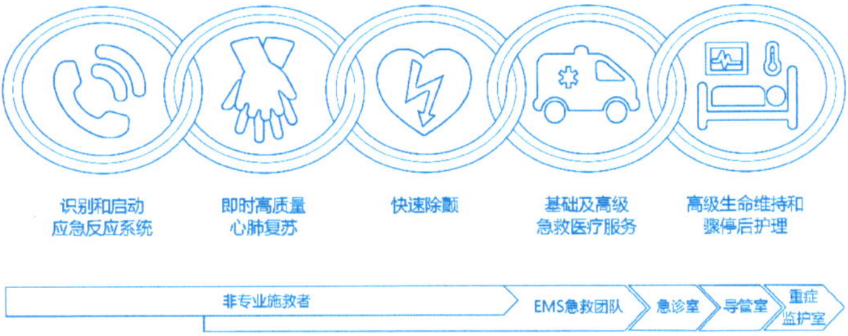


图 1　完整生存链

## 三、心肺复苏步骤

CPR 是一个连贯的、系统的急救技术，各个步骤应紧密结合、不间断地进行。心肺复苏术分为下列四个阶段。

**快速准备期：**判断病人是否发生心跳呼吸骤停，准备投入抢救；

**现场心肺复苏：**即基础生命支持 (BLS)；

**进一步心肺复苏：**即高级生命支持（ACLS）；

**后续心肺复苏：**即后续生命支持 (PLS)。

现场心肺复苏术是挽救生命的基础阶段，如果现场心肺复苏不及时，操作不正确，则将导致心肺复苏抢救的失败。现场心肺复苏的步骤如下。

1. 确认现场安全；

2. 检查是否有反应；

3. 呼叫附近人帮助抢救；

4. 检查脉搏和呼吸；

5. 胸外按压；

6. 开放气道；

7. 人工呼吸；

8. 循环胸外按压和人工呼吸；

9. 尽早使用体外自动除颤器（AED）；

10. 转送医院，继续复苏。

为方便记忆，可简称为 C、A、B、D。

**C(Compression，胸外按压)：**包含前面的评估和判断步骤，即第 1 ~ 5 项，在确保现场安全的情况下，判断病人失去反应。呼叫他人帮忙，并尽快取得 AED。评估病人失去了正常的呼吸和脉搏（非专业人员可以不检查脉搏），立刻将病人放置为仰卧位，进行胸外按压。

**A（Airway，开放气道）：**即第 6 项，采用仰头举颏法畅通呼吸道。

**B（Breath，人工呼吸）：**即第 7 项，采用口对口进行人工呼吸。在 AED 到达前，进行第 8 项，即以“胸外按压 30 次：人工呼吸 2 次”的比例循环进行。

**D（Defibrillation，除颤）：**即第 9 项，AED 到达后，立即接通 AED，分析心律，可除颤时进行除颤，并尽快进入第 10 项，转送至医院进一步复苏。

## 四、心肺复苏的简单原理

现场心肺复苏术主要为徒手操作，在许多场合下这是唯一实用的有效办法，如应用器械操作，则往往会为寻找器械而浪费许多宝贵时间。

心跳停止后，全身血液循环亦立即停止，脑组织及许多重要脏器得不到血液及氧气的供应，数分钟后就会相继出现细胞坏死。从 2010 年开始，美国心脏协会将心肺复苏的步骤从 A—B—C（气道—呼吸—胸外按压）改为 C—A—B—D（胸外心脏按压—气道—呼吸—除颤）。无反应、无呼吸的病人或呼吸异常的病人，都应当立即行胸外心脏按压，几分钟内氧气就会进入肺和血流，因此最先开始胸外按压会促进氧气更快地输送到大脑和心脏。另一方面，心跳停止初期血液中含氧量还比较高，此时循环支持比呼吸支持更重要，而且胸外按压本身也能产生一定的通气，所以开始只按压也不会立即造成机体的氧供不足。

胸外按压产生血液循环的机制有两个："胸泵机制"和"心泵机制"。

胸外按压时胸内压增高，主动脉、左心室、大静脉及食管所受压力基本相同，主动脉收缩压明显升高，血液向胸腔外动脉流去（图 2a）。在胸腔入口处的大静脉被压陷（由于静脉壁比动脉壁薄），颈静脉瓣阻止血液返流。动脉对抗血管萎陷的抗力大于静脉，且动脉管腔相对较小，等量血液在动脉中可产生较大抗力，因而动脉管腔在胸外按压时保持开放。于是在按压时血液只能从动脉向前流，不能向静脉返流。放松时（图 2b），胸内压可降至零，因而静脉壁不受压，管腔开放，血液可从静脉返回心脏；当动脉血返回心脏时，由于受主动脉瓣阻挡，血液不能返流入心腔，部分可从冠状动脉开口流入冠状动脉营养心脏，是为"胸泵机制"（图 2）。

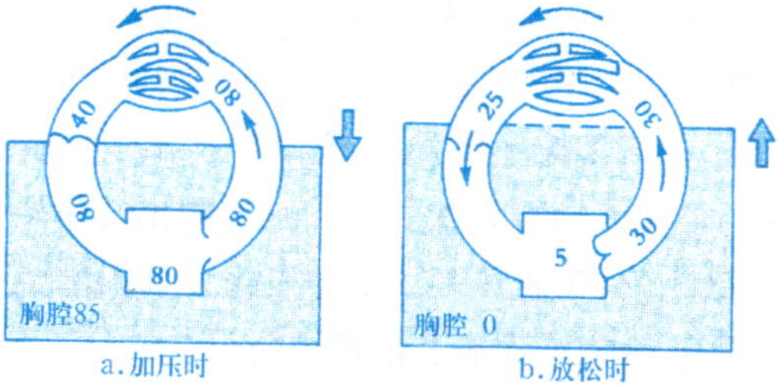


图 2　胸泵机制（压力单位为：毫米汞柱）

其次，在体格瘦小者和婴幼儿，胸外按压施加的压力，将心脏向后压于坚硬的脊柱上，使心内血液被排出，加上心脏瓣膜的作用，使血流向动脉。按压松弛时，心脏恢复原状，静脉血被动吸回心脏，是为“心泵机制”。

病人心跳呼吸停止后，全身肌肉松弛，口腔内的舌肌也松弛导致舌根后坠，因此阻塞了呼吸通路。采取头后仰，抬举下颏，可使舌根部向上提起，从而使呼吸道畅通（图 3）。

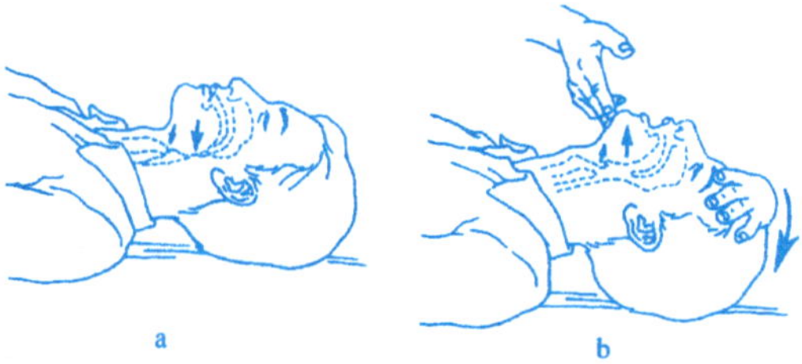


图 3　畅通呼吸道

在畅通呼吸道之后，就能用口向病人肺内顺利吹气。正常人吸入的空气含氧量为 21%，二氧化碳为 0.04%。肺脏吸收 20% 的氧气，其余 80% 的氧气按原样呼出。因此，我们正常人给病人吹气时，只要吹出气量较多（400 ~ 600 毫升），则进入病人肺内的氧气量可达 18%，基本上是够用的。

## 五、脑复苏的重要性及基本措施

心跳呼吸骤停病人要想取得复苏的成功，必须重视以脑复苏为重点的高级生命支持（ACLS）和后续生命支持（PLS）。

及时正确的 CPR，是脑复苏最初、最重要的措施之一。此外，脑复苏的基本措施还有以下几方面。

1. 维持血压：要求立即恢复并维持正常或稍高于正常的血压，要防止突然发生血压过高和预防低血压。

2. 控制呼吸：神志不清和气体交换不满意的病人，应该使用呼吸机。

3. 降温疗法：人工亚低温可降低脑代谢、减少脑耗氧，故在不影响 CPR 下，应尽早采取有效的降温措施，尤其是选择性头部低温，降温程度以达 33 ~ 34℃为宜。要坚持到皮质功能开始恢复，即出现听觉为止。

4. 渗透疗法：应用甘露醇等提高血浆渗透压以吸收血管外、细胞外水分至血管内由肾排出，用利尿剂（呋塞米等）也可降低细胞内水分。应注意使血浆渗透压维持在 > 330 毫摩 / 升。

5. 肾上腺皮质激素的应用：如地塞米松首

次 0.4 毫克 / 千克，然后 0.2 毫克 / 千克，每 6 小时一次，一般不超过 4 天。

6. 高压氧：有条件时应及早使用高压氧治疗。

7. 其他：注意水、电解质平衡，营养疗法，防止感染等。

第二章

# 现场心肺复苏的操作方法

## 一、如何识别心跳呼吸骤停

病人意识突然丧失，昏倒在地；面色苍白或转为发绀；呼吸消失或叹息样呼吸；瞳孔散大；部分病人可有短暂抽搐，伴头眼偏斜，随即全身肌肉松弛。

## 二、心肺复苏基本框架

每个人都可以成为心跳呼吸骤停的施救者，但使用这项技能取决于训练水平、经验和信心。2015 年版心肺复苏指南和 2017 年心肺复苏指南更新内容根据救援人员受训情况，将参与性 CPR 分为：调度员指导实施 CPR、旁观者实施 CPR 和急救医疗服务人员实施 CPR。

根据施救者熟练程度，实施的心肺复苏模块分为以下三个层次。

1. 单纯胸外按压心肺复苏：对于培训不足、设备有限的单名施救者可能只能提供胸外按压直到有其他帮助。

2. 30∶2 心肺复苏：施救者信心充足且训练有素，可同时提供胸外按压和急救呼吸，使用每 30 次按压接 2 次人工呼吸的比例。

3. 高效团队协作心肺复苏：一名施救者进行胸外按压，另一名施救者通过球囊给予呼吸，第三名施救者使用体外自动除颤器（AED）。

## 三、现场心肺复苏程序

### （一）确认现场安全，检查病人有无反应，并呼叫帮助

1. 确保现场对自己和病人均是安全的（图 4）。

图 4　观察周围环境

2. 检查病人有无反应，轻拍病人的肩膀，并大声呼唤：“你还好吗？”（图 5）。

图 5　判断有无意识

3. 如果病人没有反应，大声向周围人求助，指定人拨打“120”急救电话和取 AED（图 6）。

图 6　呼救

**注意事项**

一定要呼叫其他人来帮忙，因为一个人做心肺复苏术不可能坚持较长时间，而且劳累后动作不准确，影响复苏效果。要指定某个人打

"120"急救电话和取得附近的 AED，并给予反馈。

（二）同时评估脉搏和呼吸，不应超过 10 秒（图 7）

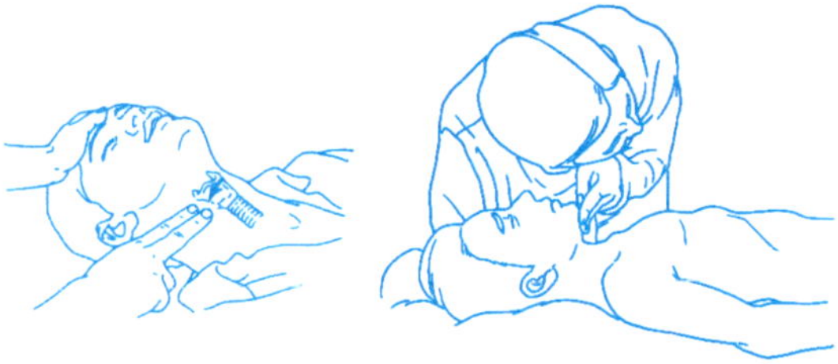

图 7　评估呼吸、脉搏

1. 检查呼吸：扫视病人胸部。如果病人有正常呼吸，你只需要陪同病人，等待"120"急救人员到达；如果病人无呼吸或仅是濒死样呼吸，是心搏骤停的标志。

2. 检查脉搏：触摸颈动脉搏动。示（食）指和中指触摸颈前气管正中（男性为喉结）旁 2 厘米，至少感觉脉搏 5 秒，但不要超过 10 秒，如果没有确切感觉到脉搏，则以胸外按压开始心肺复苏。

3. 若呼吸和脉搏都正常：如果呼吸正常且脉搏存在，陪同病人，等待"120"急救人员到达。

4. 若脉搏存在而呼吸不正常：如果病人脉搏存在，没有正常呼吸，则开放气道，单纯给予人工呼吸，并每两分钟重新评估脉搏和呼吸。

5. 若脉搏和呼吸都不正常：如果病人无正常呼吸或仅为濒死叹息样呼吸且无脉搏，要立即开始心肺复苏。

**注意事项**

◇何为濒死样呼吸？

濒死样呼吸不是正常呼吸，看起来像要迅速吸进大量空气的表现，嘴可能是打开的，下颌、头或颈部可能随着濒死叹息样呼吸移动，可能表现有力或微弱，通常频率较慢，是心搏骤停的标志。

◇不会触摸颈动脉搏动怎么办？

美国心脏协会 2015 年版和 2017 年修订的心肺复苏指南中不建议非专业人员为了明确心跳呼吸是否停止而反复触摸脉搏甚至用听诊器探测心音，以避免延误心肺复苏开始的时间。

（三）高质量心肺复苏：胸外按压、开放气道和人工呼吸

1. 病人和施救者体位摆放：确保病人仰卧在坚固平坦的平面上。施救者双膝跪在病人一侧，与病人的肩部平齐。一只手的掌根放在病人胸骨下半部（男性为两乳头连线中点），另一只手掌根重叠置于第一只手上。双手臂伸直，

靠腰部用力向下按压（图 8 和图 9）。

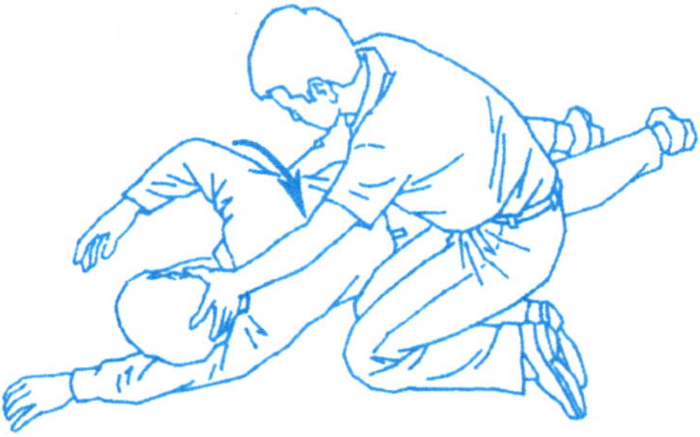

图 8　体位摆放

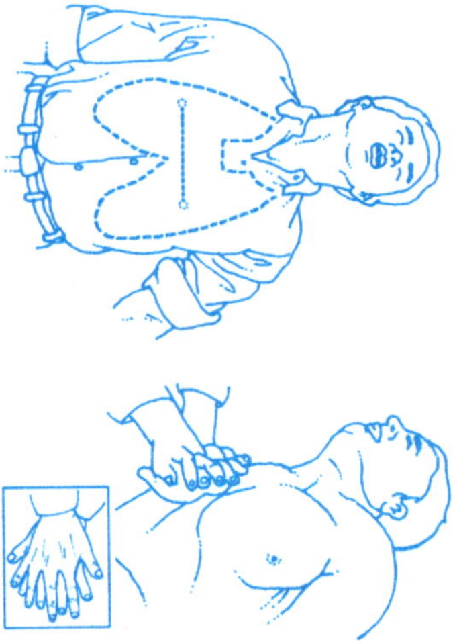

图 9　胸外按压部位和手势

2. 高质量胸外按压：按压速度为每分钟

100 ~ 120 次，按压深度为 5 ~ 6 厘米，每次按压结束后，确保胸廓完全回弹，尽量减少按压中断次数（图 10）。

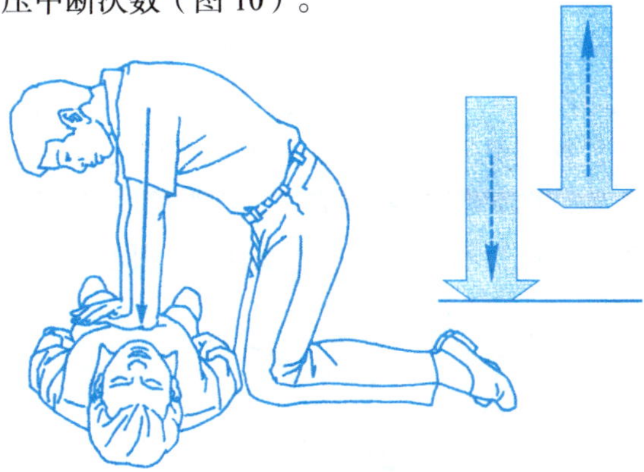

图 10　胸外按压深度

3. 仰头抬颏法开放气道：将一手置于前额使头部后仰，另一手的示(食)指与中指置于下颌骨近下颏或下颌角处，抬起下颏(图 11)。

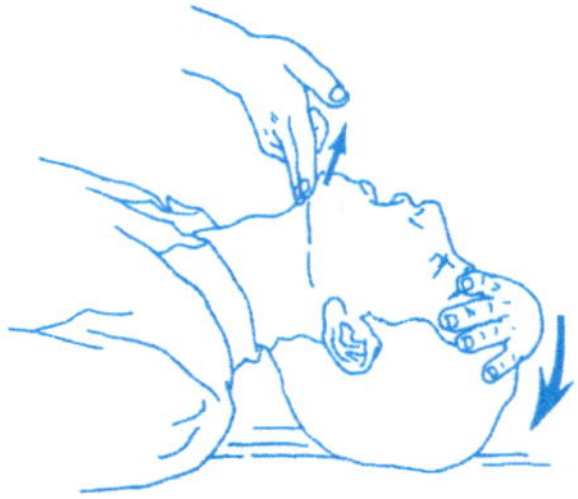

图 11　畅通呼吸道

4. 高质量人工呼吸：用按于前额的手的拇

指与示（食）指捏闭病人的鼻孔（捏紧鼻翼下端）；施救者张开嘴贴紧病人的嘴（要把病人的嘴部完全包住）；用力向病人嘴内吹气，吹气时间约为 1 秒，吹气量为 400 ~ 600 毫升，此时可观察到病人胸廓抬起。一次吹气完毕后，应放松捏鼻的手，以便病人从鼻孔呼气，此时病人胸部向下塌陷，有气流从口鼻排出。再以同样方法，进行第二次人工呼吸通气（图 12）。

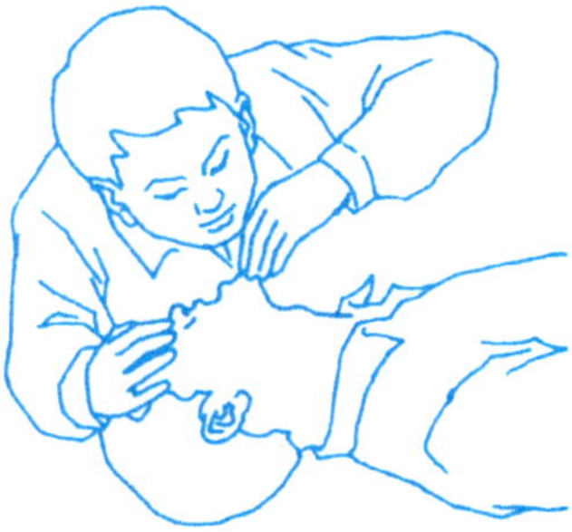

a

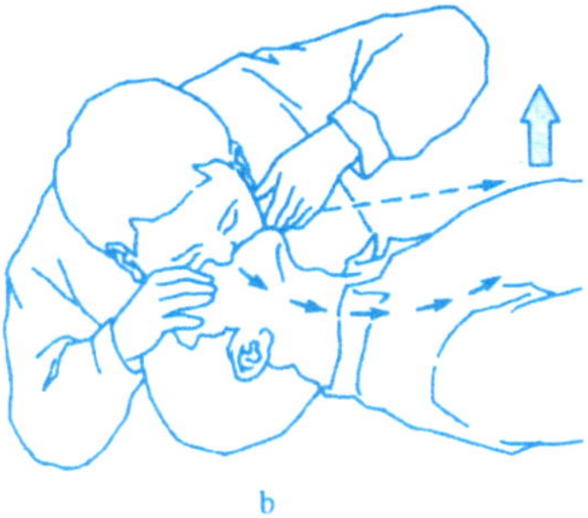

b

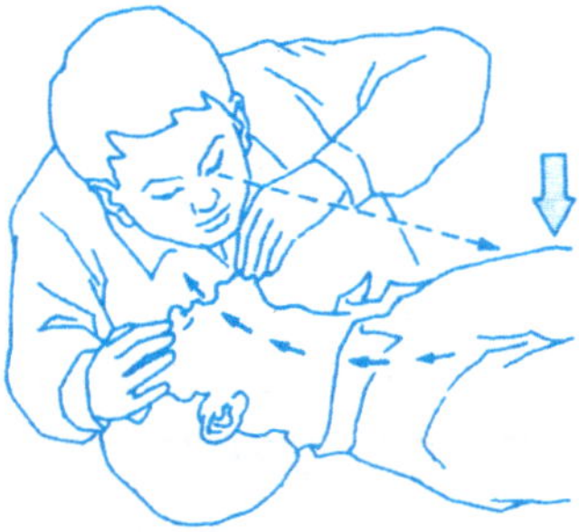

c

图 12　口对口人工呼吸

5. 胸外按压 30 次：人工呼吸 2 次循环：即每 30 次胸外按压后进行 2 次人工呼吸为一个心肺复苏循环。首轮做 5 个心肺复苏循环（即 5 个 30:2 的胸外按压和人工呼吸），历时约 2 分钟，复检呼吸、颈动脉搏动。如果没有明确地感受到脉搏，重新从胸外按压开始进行 CPR。如有 AED 在场，则启用 AED。直至出现呼吸及动脉搏动，表明心肺复苏成功，可以送至医疗机构进行进一步的救治。

**注意事项**

◇病人体位摆放有何要求？

确保病人仰卧位于坚固平面。若位于弹簧床或软沙发上，会大大削弱按压效果。如果病人俯卧，需小心将病人翻过来。如果怀疑病人有头部或颈椎损伤，将病人翻转为仰卧位时应尽量使其头部、颈部和躯干保持在一条直线上。

◇仰头举颏法开放气道需要注意什么？

不要用力按压颌下的软组织，因为这样会堵塞气道。

◇人工呼吸担心传染病怎么办？

心肺复苏的感染风险极低，若实在担心，可用简易呼吸器代替口对口呼吸，或只单纯进行胸外按压。

◇胸外按压常见的错误见于哪些情形？

（1）按压时除掌根部贴在胸骨外，手指也压在胸壁上，这容易引起骨折（肋骨或肋软骨交界处）。

（2）按压定位不正确。向下错位易使剑突受压折断而致肝破裂。向两侧错位易致肋骨或肋软骨交界处骨折，导致气胸、血胸。

（3）按压用力不垂直，导致按压无效或骨折，特别是摇摆式按压更易出现严重并发症（图 13）。

（4）抢救者按压时肘部弯曲。因而用力不够，按压深度达不到 5 ~ 6 厘米（图 14）。

（5）冲击式按压、猛压，其效果差，且易导致骨折。

（6）放松时未能使胸部充分松弛，胸部

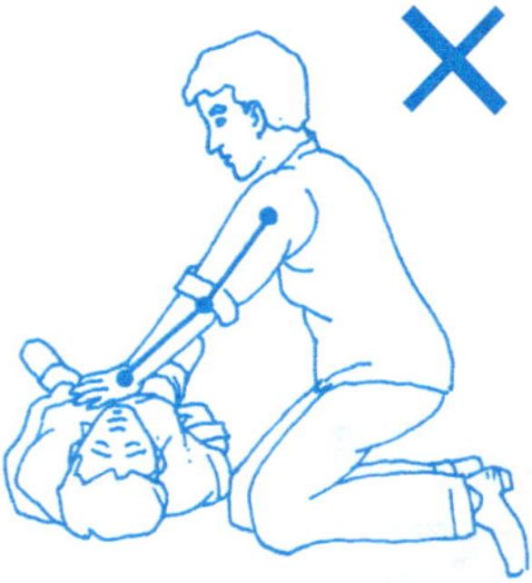

图 13　胸外按压不垂直

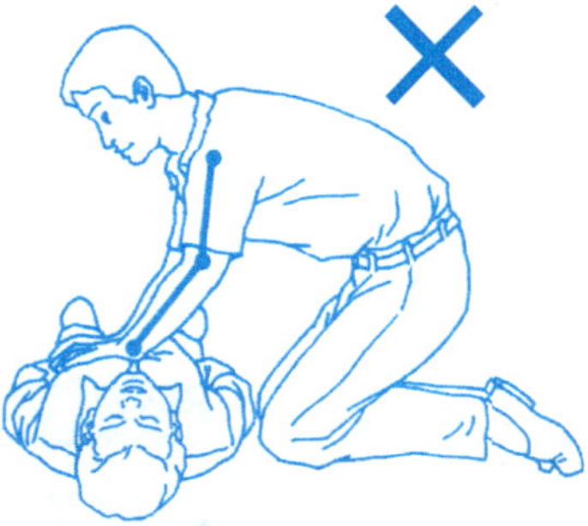

图 14　胸外按压肘部弯曲

仍承受压力，使血液难以回到心脏。

（7）按压速度不自主的加快或减慢，影响了按压效果。

（8）两手掌不是重叠放置，而呈交叉放置（图 15）。

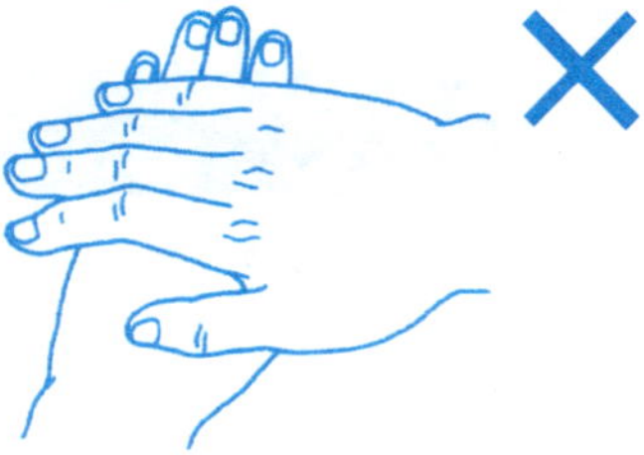

图 15　胸外按压两手掌的错误

（9）开始 2 分钟后，检查一次脉搏和呼吸。以后每 3 ~ 5 分钟检查一次，检查不超过 5 秒钟，最好由协助抢救者检查。

（10）如用担架搬运病人，应该持续做心肺复苏，中断时间不得超过10秒钟。

## 四、成人心搏骤停救治流程（图16）

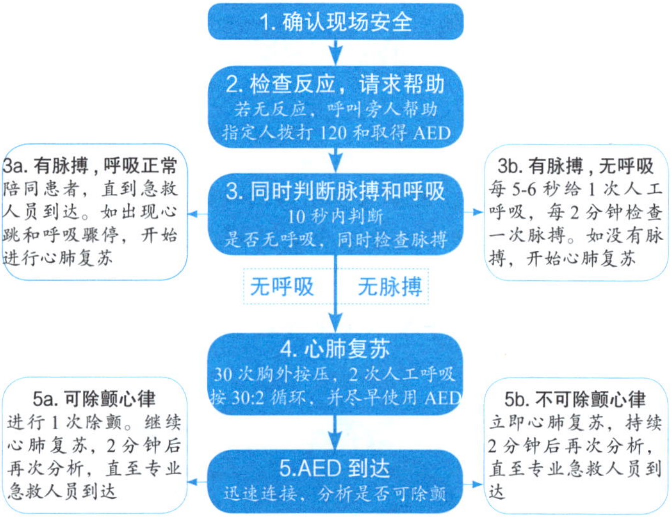


图16 成人心搏骤停救治流程

第三章

# 婴幼儿心肺复苏要点

婴儿是小于1岁，幼儿是1～3岁，在心肺复苏时，其心肺复苏处理流程基本同成人，但有以下几处特殊之处。

1. 判断有无反应：婴幼儿对言语不能反应，可轻拍婴幼儿的肩膀或脚跟，如有哭泣，则为有反应。

2. 检查脉搏和呼吸：应同时检查脉搏和呼吸。

检查婴幼儿脉搏时，因其颈部肥胖，颈动脉不易触及，可触摸肱动脉搏动。肱动脉位于上臂内侧肘和肩之间。抢救者示（食）指和中指置于上臂内侧，在肘和肩膀之间，然后按下手指尝试感受脉搏（非专业医护人员可免除这一步骤）（图17）。

检查婴幼儿呼吸时，方法同成人（见本书第14～15页）。

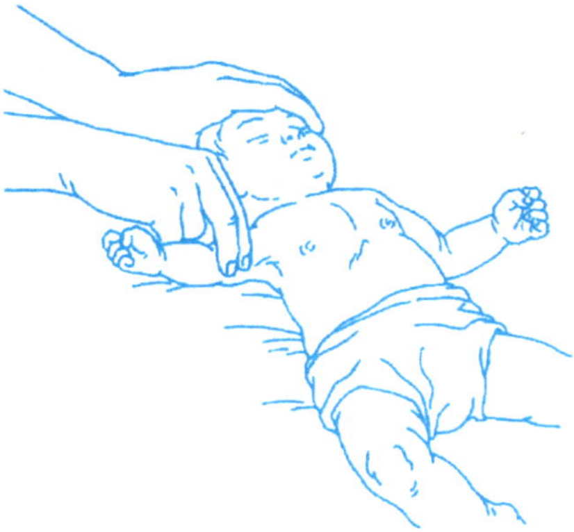

图 17 检查婴幼儿肱动脉

3. 胸外按压和人工通气。

所有心跳呼吸骤停病人按压频率均为 100 ~ 120 次 / 分。对于婴幼儿，若是单名施救者，按压 / 通气比例仍是 30 ：2；若有两名施救者，使用的按压 / 通气比例为 15：2。

对婴幼儿，按压部位是两乳头连线与胸骨正中线交界点下一横指处。将两根拇指并排放在婴幼儿胸部上述位置，对于非常小的婴幼儿，拇指可能会重叠放置。用双手的手指环绕婴幼儿的胸部，并支撑婴幼儿的背部，用两根拇指以 100 ~ 120 次 / 分的速率按压胸骨（图 18）。按压深度为婴幼儿胸廓前后径的 1/3（4 ~ 5 厘米）。

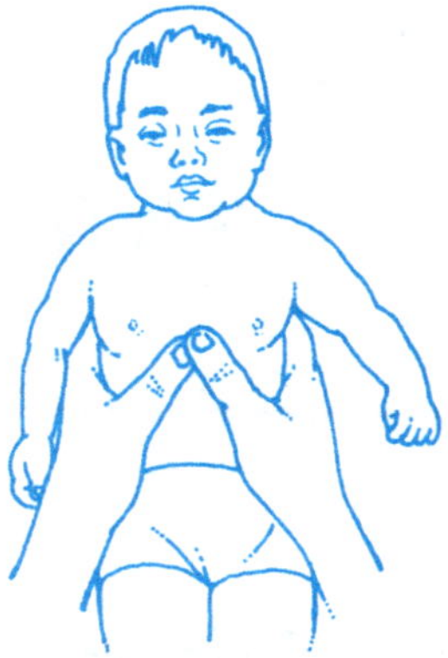

图 18 婴幼儿环抱法按压

# 第四章

# 体外自动除颤器（AED）

## 一、早期除颤的重要性

自动体外除颤器（automated external defibrillator，AED）是一种轻型便携式计算机化设备，能够识别需要电击除颤的异常心律(心室颤动或无脉性室性心动过速)，并使心律得以恢复正常。

早期除颤在复苏过程中占有重要地位，也是院外心跳呼吸骤停病人完整生存链（图 1，本书第 4 页）中的重要一环。最新的指南要求当可以立即取得 AED 时，有目击者的院外心跳呼吸骤停应当尽快使用 AED。若不能立即取得 AED 时，应该在他人前往获取以及准备 AED 时进行 CPR，而且要视病人情况，在 AED 设备可供使用后尽快尝试除颤。

**注意事项**

◇为何强调早期除颤?

（1）大部分（80% ~ 90%）成人突发、非创伤性心跳呼吸骤停的最初心律失常为室颤。

（2）除颤是对室颤最有效的治疗手段。

（3）随着时间的推移，除颤成功率会迅速下降，每推迟一分钟下降 7% ~ 10%。

（4）室颤在数分钟内转变为心搏骤停，则复苏成功的希望很小。

## 二、操作 AED 的步骤

（一）开启 AED

打开包装或盖子，按电源键开启 AED（图 19）。

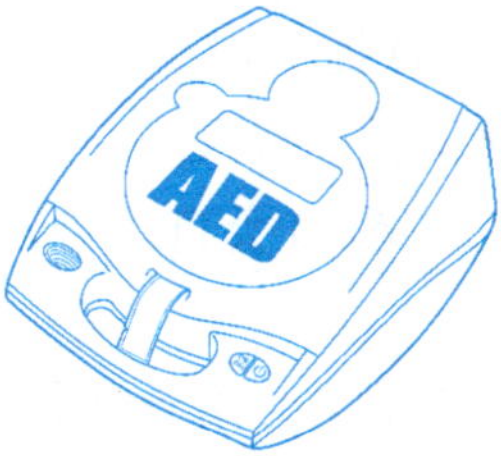


图 19

（二）贴电极片并连接 AED

1. 将 AED 电极片贴到病人裸露的胸部，按照电极片上的图片位置，通常为前侧位。一个电极片放置在右锁骨正下方，另一电极片放在左乳头外侧（图 20）。

2. 将 AED 连接电缆接到 AED 装置上。

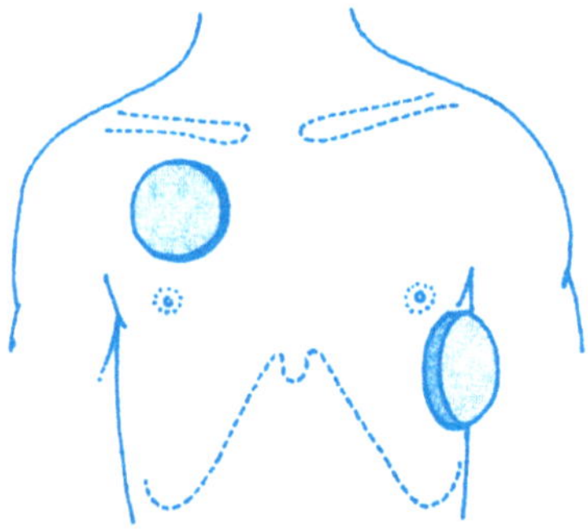

图 20 AED 电极片位置

（三）离开病人，AED 分析心律

1. 如果 AED 提示正在分析病人心律，施救者应确保无人接触病人。

2. 分析后，AED 会自动告诉你是否需要电击。

（四）离开病人，给予电击

1. 如果 AED 建议电击，在电击前应遣散周围人，确保无人接触病人，大声说“请所有人离开”。操作者环顾确认没人接触病人，按下电击按钮。

2. 如果不需电击或电击完成后，应立即从胸外按压开始进行心肺复苏。

3. 经过5个心肺复苏循环后或2分钟后，AED会自动提示重复步骤（三）和（四）。

# 第五章

# 心肺复苏有效指标和终止抢救的指征

## 一、心肺复苏有效的指标

心肺复苏术操作是否正确，主要靠平时严格训练，掌握正确的方法。而在急救中判断复苏是否有效，可以根据以下五方面综合考虑。

1. 瞳孔：复苏有效时，可见瞳孔由大变小。如瞳孔由小变大、固定，则说明复苏无效。

2. 面色（口唇）：复苏有效，可见面色由发绀转为红润；如若变为灰白，则说明复苏无效。

3. 颈动脉搏动：按压有效时，每一次按压可以摸到一次搏动，如停止按压，搏动亦消失，此时应继续进行胸外按压，如停止按压后脉搏仍然跳动，则说明病人心跳已恢复（按压有效时可测到血压在60/40毫米汞柱左右）。

4. 神志：复苏有效，可见病人眼球活动。

5. 出现自主呼吸：自主呼吸出现，并不意味着可以停止人工呼吸。如果自主呼吸微弱，仍应坚持口对口呼吸。

## 二、心肺复苏无效的指征

现场心肺复苏应持续进行，在现场抢救中不可武断地做出心肺复苏无效的判断。如有条件确定下列指征时，可考虑终止心肺复苏。

1. 脑死亡：深度昏迷，对任何刺激无反应；自主呼吸持续停止；脑干反射全部或大部分消失，包括：瞳孔对光反射、角膜反射、吞咽反射、睫脊反射（脊髓反射除外）。

2. 无心跳及脉搏。

有以上两个条件，再加上已做心肺复苏30分钟以上，可以考虑病人死亡，心肺复苏无效，可终止心肺复苏。

**注意事项**

◇现场抢救人员终止心肺复苏有哪些条件？

（1）自主呼吸及心跳已恢复良好。

（2）有其他人接替抢救，或有医生到场

承担了复苏工作。

（3）有医生到场，确定病人已死亡。

以上三个条件具备其一，现场抢救人员可考虑终止心肺复苏。

# 第六章

# 心肺复苏模型

## 一、心肺复苏模型的操作和训练

理想的心肺复苏模型应具备以下特性：①当颈部屈曲时呼吸道会阻塞；②人工呼吸及胸外按压时其胸部阻力应与人体近似；③下颌可以张合；④有指示器显示人工呼吸呼气量、胸外按压部位及幅度；⑤有颈动脉搏动装置。

目前国产和进口的 CPR 模型均以绿灯点亮与否显示人工呼吸通气量是否足够，黄灯点亮与否显示胸外按压位置及幅度是否正确，以红灯亮显示按压部位错误（图 21）。

有条件时，可增加除颤训练模型和气管插管模型，此外还有婴幼儿心肺复苏模型。

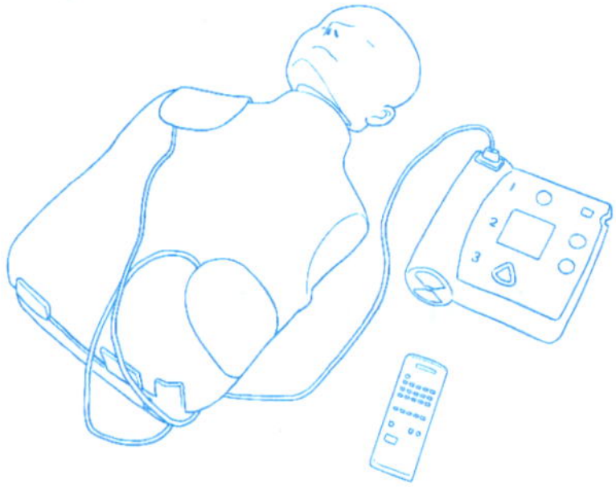

图 21　复苏模型

## 二、心肺复苏模型的消毒和保护

训练模型应有专人保管。操作训练时应将模型平放在地上或平板床上进行，训练前要认真进行消毒,尤其应对塑料肺及气道进行冲洗。可使用 75%酒精或附在模型箱内的消毒液。CPR 模型训练一般不会引起疾病传播。

## 三、心肺复苏术培训

进行心肺复苏术的培训，必须具备下列三个条件：①合格的教材。②合格的教具。③合格的教师。

Praise for *It's Only Forever*

"Jes Battis has mastered a beautiful alchemy, one which blends cultural critique with their own personal journey and also examines queerness and neurodivergence, visible in all corners of this beloved eighties film. Told in the shadows of the HIV/AIDS crisis and the current challenges bearing down on queer and trans lives, Battis reminds us to hold on to this beautiful lesson that can be learned in the darkest and scariest of places: the things that make us other are the same that give us power. *It's Only Forever* is a tender and beautiful ode to the interwoven cultural touchstones that contribute to the portrait of a life."
— Niko Stratis, author of *The Dad Rock That Made Me a Woman*

"Jes Battis takes readers on a nostalgia-laced tour of Henson's classic film filtered through queer, neurodivergent, and othered lenses. Embrace your inner goblin and dance the magic dance!"
— Joe Lipsett, film critic and podcaster

"*It's Only Forever* is my favorite kind of book, one that leaves me both giggling and sniffling, highlighting the most impactful lines. Readers will be pulled in by Jes Battis's quick wit and hilarious prose and will find themselves swirling about in truths so heavy and clear that they will become lost in their own labyrinths of nostalgia and critical reflection. Luckily, unlike many a creature in the film, Battis doesn't leave you on your own without instructions, but instead carefully unravels the complexity of Jim Henson's iconic film through a mix of

academic readings, nostalgic pop culture considerations, and little windows into their own life. For all the weird kids out there, this book will feel like coming home."

— Cassandra Ozog, co-editor of *"You're Muted": Performance, Precarity, and the Logic of Zoom*

"I thought I'd seen *Labyrinth* from every angle, but Jes Battis's thoughtful meditation has uncovered new pathways into the film. Like Sarah's journey, this book is a reexamination of the ever-shifting nature of dreams, sexual impulses, and the goblins who pursue us, or the goblins we secretly long to join. As a work of art, *Labyrinth* has always been generous in offering plenty of room for interpretation, and Battis accepts the film's invitation with vulnerability and insight, drawing on personal memories that shed new light on the importance of exploring mazes. Analytical, intimate, and queer in every sense of the word, this book feels like a natural extension of the nostalgic mental roaming that fans of the film have been happily indulging in for the last forty years."

— Matt Baume, author of *Hi Honey, I'm Homo! Sitcoms, Specials, and the Queering of American Culture*

## the pop classics series

**#1** *It Doesn't Suck.*
*Showgirls*

**#2** *Raise Some Shell.*
*Teenage Mutant Ninja Turtles*

**#3** *Wrapped in Plastic.*
*Twin Peaks*

**#4** *Elvis Is King.*
*Costello's My Aim Is True*

**#5** *National Treasure.*
*Nicolas Cage*

**#6** *In My Humble Opinion.*
*My So-Called Life*

**#7** *Gentlemen of the Shade.*
*My Own Private Idaho*

**#8** *Ain't No Place for a Hero.*
*Borderlands*

**#9** *Most Dramatic Ever.*
*The Bachelor*

**#10** *Let's Go Exploring.*
*Calvin and Hobbes*

**#11** *Extra Salty.*
*Jennifer's Body*

**#12** *Right, Down + Circle.*
*Tony Hawk's Pro Skater*

**#13** *The Time of My Life.*
*Dirty Dancing*

**#14** *Clever Girl.*
*Jurassic Park*

**#15** *Ugh! As If!*
*Clueless*

**#16** *It Can't Rain All the Time.*
*The Crow*

**#17** *It's Only Forever.*
*Labyrinth*

# Contents

## **Introduction: *Labyrinth and the Spectacle of Growing Up***

It's 1986 and I'm in the Paramount Theatre in Chilliwack with my dad, waiting for *Labyrinth* — and life — to start. I'm eight years old, and my parents are freshly divorced. Eight is a weird age, because you can sense all kinds of tectonic shifts in the social world around you, but you're not always sure what they mean. Your parents seem to share a single story, until it's suddenly difficult to remember the last time they occupied a room together. I know that my dad lives in a snug one-bedroom apartment, where I sleep on a foam mattress like an awkward Cinderella. I know that my mom works at a record store during the day and a club called Earthquake Annie's at night.

Here are a few things that I don't know yet:

My brain is wired like this crumbling theater, where the lights sometimes flicker and the golden curtain gets stuck halfway down.

There's a reason I feel more like myself in the dark.

A movie about a suburban teen white girl, a maze full of goblins, and David Bowie in a feather cloak is about to change my life.

Already I'm no beginner when it comes to eighties fantasy cinema. I've seen both *The Neverending Story* and *Legend*, which we'll talk about later as two parts (with *Labyrinth* as the third) of a holy trinity. My dad's postdivorce parenting contribution is taking me to matinées, so I have already learned that I need a luck dragon, and that — maybe — I want to dance to a Tangerine Dream song with Tim Curry in devil horns. But I'm not sure this can really prepare me for *Labyrinth*.

The lights go down.

A silver owl flies across a glowing blue maze.

The owl is both real and not. I'm not sure I can trust what I'm seeing, and that's an extension of my feeling of moving through the world as a kid — very little makes sense. This cinematic and intimate moment is also the birth of CGI and my awareness of special effects, and the whole movie will hesitate between tones: light and shadow, safe and dangerous, real and not real.

*

Many classic films sound ridiculous when you try to offer a logical synopsis. *It's about a giant man-eating plant and everyone's sort of gay. It's about an evil professor from transsexual Transylvania who has the misfortune of falling in love. It's about a fat kid who's consumed by grief over the death of his mother, and he thinks if he reads the correct magic book, she'll be fine and not dead.* Trying to summarize *Labyrinth* results in similar problems.

It's about:

> A girl who hates her stepbrother, and by extension, the woman in pearls who's replaced her mother.
>
> A shape-shifting demi-human, played by a famously bisexual artist, who is probably centuries old and wants to trap her forever.
>
> The intolerable pain of growing up, and wondering if you could just live in a dancing crystal.
>
> The seductive queer life of goblins, who can be hairy giants, sassy doorknobs, balls of flame, wandering hags, or everything you've ever wanted.

By the end of the film, when Sarah defeats the Goblin King, I feel a piercing sadness, because now she has to go back to her regular life. She will date boys and go to prom (which

I barely understand at the time, but filmmaker John Hughes seems to find it important), and she'll grow up to look exactly like her stepmother in shades of beige. Her shaggy dog, Merlin, is just a regular dog again, who will get regular cancer one day, and no spell will save him. I want Sarah to hold on to her difference — our difference — to transcend the boundaries of the everyday world, and it's not *fair* that she has to be like everyone else.

But in the final scene, just as Sarah faces down her regular life once again, her toys come alive. Because they're needed. She dances in her mundane bedroom with a crowd of beasts like the sisters in Christina Rossetti's poem "Goblin Market," and it seems possible that a sliver of weird, gold-drenched life could also be running parallel to my uncomfortable current world. I know I'm queer in the way children know this. I know I'd rather be a bird than a boy. I know my brain is wired differently, something I told my mom when I was six. Until now, I haven't known what to do with this information.

Maybe I will simply become a goblin. I imagine joining a wild rumpus in my bedroom with the weird and furry creatures who only need to understand the quixotic rules of their own society.[1] They get to live underground, in quiet and dark places, where I wouldn't have to worry about my dim understanding of AIDS, or the Iran-Contra affair, or Ronald Reagan's space lasers. Down there, there's always a deeply hidden tunnel, always a way out.

---

1 *Rumpus* has a weird etymology — related to "romp" — but it probably comes from the Latin *rompere*, "to break through," which feels fitting.

*Labyrinth*, with unhinged, wild plot twists and characters, proposes a number of fascinating escapes. But it's also about a wealthy, white suburban teen whose room is full of fantasy merchandise. It's about a girl who decides that her power lies in going home, not staying to rule the underground that's offered to her. I would never be Sarah — that was a painful lesson.

But I could, maybe, come close to ruling my own underground.

We all can, and that's what this book is about.

*Labyrinth* keeps offering us something even as the world falls down.

## THE DRAMA OF BEING HUMAN

*Labyrinth* was the first real *spectacle* that I remember seeing in a movie theater. I'd loved both *Legend* and *The Neverending Story*, but *Labyrinth* was a sensorium that devoured me from every angle. There were monsters, and computer graphics, and lush synth music, and dancing crystals that remembered your dreams, and sets that were nearly postapocalyptic, and rapid-fire jokes courtesy of screenwriter Terry Jones, and of course, there was Bowie.

The first scene where Jareth appears to Sarah in a feather cloak, offering a twisted bargain — "Just fear me, love me, do as I say, and I will be your slave" — fundamentally altered my DNA as a queer eight-year-old who already wanted to escape the sensory world. (I didn't understand the coercive tone of

this scene at first — more on that later.) It just seemed like Bowie was offering a world of owls and goblins and impossible staircases, a world where you could be anything you wanted: a worm, a king, a squirrel knight, a rolling stone, a ball of flame. His tattered lace and glittering wig, so unlike my baggy sweatshirts, held the promise of a wild, unexpected gender. And wasn't being lost in the labyrinth far better than hiding in the bathroom at school, because the fluorescent lights and press of bodies made me want to crawl out of my own skin? The film promised an underground life that was crystalline and magical. I wanted to live inside that uncanny glass, hidden from everyone but my loyal band of goblins, and perhaps, an unsettling, genderfluid monarch.

The plot of *Labyrinth* was poured like molten magic into my brain at an impressionable age. But many readers may be more familiar with the *vibe* of *Labyrinth* than its actual story. A 14-year-old, Sarah, is annoyed by the lack of magic in her eighties suburban neighborhood. She goes to the nearby park with her sheepdog, Merlin, and reads a dramatic monologue from a book also called *Labyrinth*, which seems, like *The Neverending Story*, to contain whole invisible worlds. Sarah's biological mom is out of the picture,[2] and her stepmother is all wrong: she wears pearls and has a tight perm. She just wants Sarah to go on boring dates and to watch her baby brother, Toby, but all he does is cry. He's not magical at all — just an

2 There's a photo of a woman — presumably an actress — taped to Sarah's mirror, and she's posing with David Bowie. This has generated fan theories about how Sarah's mother left the family to pursue acting, though her departure is never explained in the film.

interloper in a striped onesie. This babysitting is seriously cutting into her daydreaming time, but on a deeper level, she also has no idea how to process her new blended family. Everything is changing, and she has no power to stop it.

In a moment of teenage fury, she remembers a character from her book — The Goblin King — who steals children. This may not be an ethical solution to her problem, but it's definitely a permanent one.

She cries out: *Take this screaming child far away from me!* This is the double-edged wish that we see in so many fairy tales, amplified to a spectacular level. But a funny thing happens when Sarah pours out all of her dramatic energy.

Nothing. At least, as far as Sarah can see. The audience sees a flipside reality, an underground, where goblin puppets wait gleefully for her to cast this spell. But they're disappointed. "Those aren't the words," they say to each other, holding their breaths, waiting.

Finally, in a moment of resignation, Sarah cuts through the drama and speaks directly to her own sense of pain and injustice as a teenager: *I wish the Goblin King* would *take you away. Right now.*

An owl bursts through the window of the nursery, bringing a storm of wit and gender confusion with it: David Bowie as Jareth, the Goblin King. He looks like a new-wave fantasy in leather pants, lace, and a feather cloak. He stands yet seems to be swaggering at the same time; he is a living smirk, beautiful and fearsome. Sarah's the one who summoned him, but now, he appears to hold all the power. And a contract for her baby brother.

Fairy tales love impossible rules, and *Labyrinth* is no different. Here we see that the real drama comes from making a choice, whether or not the choice is a wise one. Sarah is vulnerable: her desire has been revealed, and it's monstrous, motivated by resentment and frustration, not love or empathy. Being a teen girl is revealed as a dangerous balancing act between deferral and peace, and power and revenge. Sarah has chosen power, and the result is what comes next.

Sarah quickly learns from Jareth that she has 13 hours to find her baby brother in the castle at the heart of the labyrinth, or else he'll be a goblin forever. Jareth doesn't think that Sarah is up to it — he's the Minotaur, and she's no Theseus. But what he doesn't yet know is that you can never underestimate how powerful a teen girl can be. After all, in the myth of the Minotaur and the Cretan labyrinth, it's also a teen girl, Ariadne, who solves the puzzle.

Sarah accepts the Goblin King's challenge, and the world begins to fall down.

*

Fairy tales offer lessons, and in the process, they subject humans to all kinds of dark horrors. They shake the box of humanity to see what fears and desires might fall out. Like Gretel and Little Red Riding Hood, Sarah is armed with bravery and cleverness. Unlike them, she also has the perspective of a firmly middle-class white teenager. Her room is full of books, toys, and board games. She loves to read, perform, and problem-solve. Imagine

if Penelope from *The Odyssey*, cleverly unraveling her tapestry of suitors, had also understood how to operate a VCR. Sarah is well-prepared for this maze, or at least she thinks she is.

One of Henson's lessons that we learn through Sarah is this: We're so focused on finding the heart of a labyrinth or whatever end goal we are rushing toward, we forget about the essentially human experience of being lost, the spectacle of our own choices, good and bad, growing like a hedge maze around us.

A funny thing happens to Sarah when she first enters this particular labyrinth.

She nearly solves it.

In a scene that has spawned countless tattoos, Sarah encounters a small, blue-haired worm in a natty red scarf who claims to have a "missus" at home. The worm's name is William, though worms are intersex, so the idea of William being married to a wife remains curious. They are, at the very least, a t4t couple. In any case, William invites Sarah in for a "nice cup of tea," but when she asks for more information about the Goblin King, she's disappointed. William responds: "I'm just a worm," a statement that implies that worms can't know anything important. But they do advise Sarah that "things aren't always what they seem in this place," prompting her to look more carefully at the seemingly solid brick walls around her. Soon enough, she discovers a hidden passageway. Just as she's about to head confidently in her chosen direction, William cries out: "Don't go *that* way! *Never* go *that* way!" Sarah thanks William for the correction, and she takes the opposite path.

Unaware of Sarah's goal, William shivers and says to the audience: *If she'd have kept on going down* that *way*, *she'd have gone straight to that castle.*

This bit of dialogue is Terry Jones at his finest, playing with the viewer while reinforcing William's claim that *things aren't always what they seem*. Sarah is so close to solving this fiendish puzzle at the very start, and a random conversation with a Cockney worm, who is evidently afraid of the Goblin King, sends her in the wrong direction entirely. She will meet sarcastic door knockers, dangerous hands, slightly homicidal dancing phoenixes, a hairy monster, an old woman peddling memories, and a Quixotic squirrel knight — all because of this chance encounter with one of the labyrinth's smallest homeowners. We could say that William tries to save her from the perils of the Goblin City, and beyond it, Jareth's freaky M.C. Escher castle. After all, she's a nice girl who doesn't need that sort of aggravation.

But one of *Labyrinth*'s overarching themes is the puzzle of being human, and the many ways humans fail to accurately communicate. At the end of the day, the film isn't really about solving the labyrinth, because Sarah has to move through it in order to understand what she actually wants. Like a poem, the labyrinth isn't something to be solved — it's something to feel through to unpeel layers of meaning. In the film podcast *You Are Good*, Sarah Marshall notes: "As people, we have a weird relationship with labyrinths. They're scary, but they're comforting in a way. They offer us shelter." Jareth's labyrinth gives Sarah an architecture of feeling — a way to process what

Henson thought of as the dark heart of childhood, with its joys and catastrophes.

There are goblins, and monsters, and hungry fairies, and sarcastic doors, and sub-basements of anxiety, and queer flames that invite us to dance with them. *Labyrinth* understands that the passageway from childhood to adulthood is genuinely frightening, and there's no trick to negotiate it. Like Sarah, we just have to make choices.

Let's follow her in. There's still a bit of light. As the vast doors close behind us, what do we feel? Excitement? Mild terror? Curiosity? Regret?

All we can do is move forward.

# 1

## *Labyrinth* and Queer Amazement

What is a labyrinth, exactly? And why do we keep returning to this particular idea of wandering within a complex structure? Arguably, the maze itself is a character in *Labyrinth*, constantly shifting around Sarah as she tries to reach its mysterious heart. There are tiny goblins living beneath the pavement squares, who fuzzy up any attempt to record her progress, and wild fairies who have a surprisingly painful bite. The experience of being lost is painful and human — if you've ever been lost as an adult, the experience might be accompanied by an ugly rush of shame. *Aren't you a little too old for this?*

When our supercomputer phones have GPS systems and interactive maps, it seems impossible to actually *be* lost. But it happens all the time. I visited Dublin with my mother and found that my phone's GPS was constantly bewildered by the

town's maze of medieval alleys, lanes, and streets that seemed to snake around each other. I was often flummoxed, and it felt doubly embarrassing, since I was the younger, more capable person who was supposed to be guiding us. My mother was rarely anxious about it, though. She liked wandering. But there's a difference between vagabonding through a wonderful city and wandering fruitlessly through a maze designed to frustrate you.

So why do we keep crossing and re-crossing this labyrinthine image? What do mazes offer us, other than the chance to feel a bit of light panic in a cornfield?

## LABYRINTHS IN MYTH AND HISTORY

The archetypal labyrinth comes to us through the myth of the Cretan Minotaur. Pasiphae, the wife of King Minos, decides to sleep with a bull. And not just that — she asks the inventor Daedalus to build her a giant cow structure in which she will hide, so that she and the bull can experience a sort of erotic turducken. Afterward, she gives birth to the Minotaur, and Minos enlists Daedalus once again to build a labyrinth-prison for this half-human creature (really, if anyone's at fault here, it's Daedalus for being too indiscriminate a contractor). Theseus, a hot prince, is chosen to wander the maze under the threat of being devoured by the Minotaur, who is, of course, hungry. But Ariadne, a clever princess, falls in love with Theseus and gives him two secret weapons to be used against the Minotaur:

a clew, or ball of string (which is where we derive the word *clue*), and a massy ball of pitch. Theseus uses the string to record his progress and the ball of pitch to clog the Minotaur's ravenous mouth, which allows him to slay the monster.

Ancient Roman authors loved the myth of the Cretan labyrinth, because it had a bit of everything — puzzles, bestiality, and hot people making questionable decisions. Virgil, who we might think of as imperial Rome's poet laureate, described the labyrinth as *hic labor ille domus*: "that house of toil." Solving the labyrinth always required work, and the stakes were high — death by Minotaur. Virgil's poetic successor, Ovid — most known for bringing the gods down to earth by showing them as messy and human — described the labyrinth as *multiplique domo caecisque*[3]: "a folded house, full of blind corners." You can't just wander through this type of maze. You first have to work toward its center and work against its many traps and illusions.

Medieval cathedrals often house images of labyrinths, which appear on seals on the nave or ceiling, and which historians have tried to interpret over time. In *The Idea of the Labyrinth*, Penelope Doob notes that these "serve as emblems of magnificent design"[4] and compare the architecture of churches with the Cretan labyrinth. But they also likely symbolized Christ descending into hell, which was often described as mazelike in its infernal structure. In the fourth canto of

3 Grammar nerd moment: the -que suffix serves as an alternate form of "and" in Latin, joining "folds" and "blind corners" together across space — a bit like a guide through a labyrinth.

4 Dood, 123.

Dante's *Inferno*, the speaker describes hell as "a valley, dark and deep and filled with mist . . . I was unable to discern a thing."[5] He needs the spirit of Virgil to guide him through hell's many twists and turns.

I was chuffed to encounter, in Dood's book, a record about labyrinths from a medieval church in Auxerre. During Easter, the dean would dance in the center of the labyrinth symbol, which was inscribed into the floor. He'd hold a clew ball to symbolize the Cretan myth, while everyone joined hands to circle him. The dance was called a *tripudium*, a Roman dance that was surprisingly energetic — far more exciting than anything I experienced while attending church in my hometown. This connection across time, and across spiritual traditions, reveals the enduring power of the labyrinth as a symbol. If we could watch this dance now, we'd be literally amazed, which is the root word of *maze*. Lost in astonishment.

I once wandered through a hedge maze at an English manor house, with my partner at the time. We were hot and tired and overstimulated, barely speaking, though in a picture that they took, I'm smiling. You can't see how much I'm sweating or feel the ache of my feet. That trip to London was complex, because they were reconsidering their career path, and I was dealing with largely untreated depression and anxiety. We shared a micro-flat in Holborn, a tiny apartment that was probably older than the city where I currently live. It had a giant key that you had to turn twice, with a loud *thunk*.

5 Dante, *Commedia*.

At the time, we were making slow progress through our own emotional labyrinths. We'd argue during the day, then share a pint in the evening at the Princess Louise pub, trying to smooth things over. The highlight of our trip was when we had our own magical private dance to Cher, until the music got so loud that a neighbor pounded on our door.

I thought about how many feet had danced on those floorboards; living in a city as old as London made me feel insignificant but also electrified by possibility. I was Sarah at the start of her journey, mired in frustration but still quietly surprised when I learned to look at the walls in a different way.

## AMAZINGLY QUEER

Before seeing *Labyrinth*, my main exposure to David Bowie had been shimmying with my mom to the album *Let's Dance*. It was not an album that Bowie particularly enjoyed making, but it captured a crystalline eighties sound that has made it practically immortal. I remember sliding across the hardwood of our old bungalow in Chilliwack as my mom spun Bowie and Blondie records, the joy of "Modern Love" cascading through our tiny house, the first place she'd been able to rent on her own after the divorce.

When I look back on this era through the nostalgia of damaged-forties-adulthood, I have to admit that it was a time of wildness. There were gilded highs and catastrophic lows. My struggles with communication were becoming more visible, and

I was already coping with health issues that would put me at a social remove from other kids. But there was also dancing, and adventures in the garden overgrown with skunk cabbage, and trips to the corner store where I could read *Silver Surfer* comics and nobody asked me to move along. I identified strongly with an alien from the planet Zenn-La who served a world-eating boss and found human interactions to be, for the most part, deeply confusing. I didn't have a cosmic surfboard, but I could slip across that hardwood as if no gravity held me in place.

Bowie is understood to be a queer icon, though media critics have often struggled to define his queerness. If, like me, your introduction to Bowie was *Labyrinth*, it would be difficult to say: "This performer seems heterosexual." He wears leather pants, lace tops, and feathered cloaks. His hair is aggressively teased and highlighted. He sings and dances to an audience of goblins. He may be auditioning Sarah for the role of queen, but ultimately, he seems more interested in hosting masquerade balls. Plus, it just doesn't seem possible for Bowie to play a straight role, given the already-vibrant place he had within the queer community of the time.

Several actors were considered for the role of Jareth, including Kevin Kline (imagine how creepy he would have been — like a Gothic Willy Wonka with Shakespearean pronunciation). Bowie gave the movie mass appeal, but he also served to amplify the beautiful weirdness of the story. When your main characters are monsters and shape-shifting puppets with a fine-tuned sense of irony, it's impossible to tell a straitlaced story, and Jim Henson never tried; in fact, he has

always mined that essential layer of oddness within his films and shows. I've come to think of his creations as *amazingly queer*. They draw our eye to what's different and challenge us at times, illuminating what their home territory is, which is a kind of queer joy. David Bowie was a perfect fit.

A question I've asked over the course of my life, which may sound absurd, is *Did you want to date the Goblin King, or did you want to* be *him?*

As a partner, Jareth is full of red flags. He's controlling, arrogant, sadistic at times, deceptive, and coercive, and he refuses to take responsibility for his labyrinth's crumbling ecosystem. He definitely has an avoidant conflict style and is the type of boyfriend who would vanish into a crystal orb whenever you needed to talk about something. But he's also delightfully enigmatic, powerful, sexy, and dangerously charming. Eighties cartoons taught me that evil was ugly: Skeletor, Hordak, Mumm-Ra, that guy from the *Dungeons & Dragons* cartoon with one fashionable horn. Jareth was more of a puckish force, someone who'd kiss you and then ruin your life. *Fear me*, he tells Sarah. I was already afraid of virtually everything, and this seemed like an excellent deal. You could dwell in the enchanted labyrinth forever, and all you had to do was obey this impossibly hot demigod with fear and reverence? Sign me up. I've always been the target audience for fairy-tale contracts.

But a part of me also wanted to inhabit Jareth's complex body. He could be anything he wanted: an owl, a goblin, an old woman, a crystal ball. He was, in a sense, the whole labyrinth, and if I had to define his gender, I'd say it was . . . feathery?

The texture of moss with eye stalks? A dancing ball of flame? A shadow becoming a snake becoming a goblin? Jareth is continually transitioning throughout the film, and nothing binds him to the eighties sense of "man," which, as Jen Sookfong Lee argues in *Gentlemen of the Shade*, could essentially be summed up by the characters in *Top Gun*. Except . . . there's that volleyball scene.

*Labyrinth* is, in some ways, all volleyball scene: a two-hour interruption of toxic eighties masculinity that presents, instead, a chaotic and beautiful and femme version of fairy-tale gender. Is uncanny vaudeville a gender category? The Goblin King is, as far as we can tell, an immortal monarch who just wants to throw fancy parties and revel in the magical power of choreography. He can be sullen, vindictive, jealous, capricious, like the fairy king Oberon in *A Midsummer Night's Dream*, who rolls his eyes at mortals but also keeps making out with them.

Jareth was a constant party, and I was searching for the spell that would allow me to be a proper social being. More than that, I wanted something from gender that I couldn't fully understand at the time, but Bowie/Jareth seemed to have it. What did that kid want? Not androgyny, or not exactly. Not drag. Something liquid, something like the underside of a feather. I wanted to glide on the wings of the sorceress from *He-Man* and dance with nonbinary goblins in an eternal bedroom. What drew me most to Jareth wasn't his shifting masc/femme sides, but his transformations. He was in a state of glorious transition, and maybe that was what I wanted. To burn in gender's flame like a medieval phoenix, and never arrive

at a fixed form. Is *crystal ball* a gender? What about *floating staircases*?

I wanted a labyrinth full of genders. And it seemed so close. Like Sarah, all I had to do was betray my family and step into the dark. Wouldn't it be worth it?

I'm still not sure.

## BOWIE AND THE MAGIC OF MEMORY

There's a photo of me crying in a David Bowie shirt.

I'm six years old, and my parents are getting divorced, though I'm not sure how clearly I understand this. Mostly, they just seem to be in different places all the time. My dad is forever mowing the lawn, going for walks, or building elaborate art pieces in the garage. He's always loved the idea of bricolage — putting disparate things together. My mom spends most of her time smoking in the kitchen, clipping coupons, and — I realize now — preparing for the financial disaster of single motherhood. She will take on two jobs, working day and night, surviving on cheese sandwiches and a brand of eighties popcorn called Crunch 'n Munch. A teenage rock band will move into the basement, and I'll learn how to play the drums. But none of that has happened yet. There's just my mother inside, my father outside. And me, standing in my Bowie shirt, my first meltdown caught on camera.

You can't quite tell that I'm crying in the photo, but if you look closely, it becomes more obvious. Plus, I was there.

I remember it, though not, years later, what I was actually crying about. My dad is wearing, improbably, a cowboy hat and denim shirt. He's kneeling, and his hand is on my shoulder. I'm looking down and seem to be dissolving into the caramel-colored wall of our house on Lewis Street. Dry grass between my toes. David Bowie's blond hair is electric. His face is caught in a grid, because the eighties loved geometric prints. Maybe it was the rise of the computer age. Maybe we just wanted lines to contain everything we were feeling but couldn't say.

The mystery of this photo is who took it.

My dad was, and still is, a photographer. He's owned a number of cameras over the years, and I inherited my love of photography from him. Wherever we went, he was arranging shots, using timers and tripods. I keep telling him that he'd love Instagram, but he prefers the reassuring weight of a camera in his hands. My boyfriend also dislikes Instagram — *the formatting is all wrong* — and there are times when I can see how these two men are curiously similar. A fact that I, like most adults in therapy, try not to think about.

But who took the photo?

Was it my mother? She knew how to use a camera, but it was never her preference. My dad was the archivist of our experiences. His photographs were so clear that you could mistake them for memories, which, I suppose, we do anyway. Our brains often can't tell the difference between the picture and the event, because they live side by side. I want to believe that I remember this moment, but the reason for my crumbling expression is gone. In his children's classic *The Little*

*Prince*, Antoine de Saint-Exupéry says: *It's a secret place, the land of tears.*[6]

## SARAH AND THE RIDDLE OF REALNESS

When we first meet Sarah in *Labyrinth*, she's acting out a dramatic monologue in a suburban park. The perspective is deliberately confusing, because we've just followed an early-CGI owl through the credits, winding its way among the blue walls of the labyrinth. This film, like *The Last Starfighter* and *Flight of the Navigator*, was one of the first to use computer graphics in such a central way. The owl wasn't just a blip on the screen — it was our guide throughout the entire credit sequence. When it transitioned, in a storm of wings, to a flesh-and-blood owl, I remember feeling shock in the theater. What was real? What was illusion? This was the beginning of our love affair with augmented reality.

Sarah doesn't realize that the owl is watching her. It's one of the Goblin King's many forms, but there's a nod to Arthurian literature, as well. Her loyal sheepdog is named Merlin, and the absent-minded enchanter in T.H. White's *The Sword in the Stone* has a pet owl named Archimedes. This owl is cranky, and shits all over Merlin's magical workshop, but the owl in *Labyrinth* is snow-white and elegant, watching an awkward but

6 de Saint-Exupéry, 21.

still flawlessly pretty teenage girl who, like Taylor Swift, recites poetry alone because she has no friends.

This was another thing that drew me to Sarah. The girls that I'd seen in films like *Sixteen Candles* and even *Fast Times at Ridgemont High* were in complex relationships with their friends. They were often in a web of social relations that I barely understood, especially at that feral age, when I could barely speak to anyone. But Sarah was alone. Like a girl in a fairy tale, she faced the forest on her own terms, without anyone's help. In the opening scene, it's clear she prefers an empty park and a canine audience to the trappings of her comfortable home. A thing that I was about to lose, though I didn't quite know it yet.

In the middle of her incantation to the goblin king in her book — a soliloquy designed to break his own spell — the real-life rain begins to pour down.

Sarah wails: *It's not fair!*

This will become a refrain throughout the film. As she moves deeper into the labyrinth, Sarah comes to realize that life is crucially unfair. She learns, with the help of a monstrous menagerie, how to deal with this sharp reality of being human, to balance the unfairness of circumstance and curse with the pressing need to solve problems or, in this case, to solve the labyrinth. But does she ever really accept the inevitability of unfairness? After all, she ends the film by achieving the best of both worlds. Sarah seems to have found a loophole. She grows up, but she still gets to keep that queer magic.

Maybe that, ultimately, is what's not fair. Because who else gets such a deal?

Queerness can mean weirdness, a delight in the strange, a wrong turn that ends up being right. Sarah always felt queer to me, because she was cut off from other people her age. She chose books and riddles over dates. If Sarah is in love with anything, it's stories. And part of her power is that she *wants* to be different. She runs through suburban streets in a storm. She tells her dad to go away, while clutching a beloved toy. In an elaborate tracking shot that moves across her room, we see a book filled with playbills and promo materials that belonged to her mother, presumably an actress. In another shot, the nameless woman is posing with Bowie in a framed photo, just to add another meta layer of lush fantasy to the scene. As a protagonist, Sarah has drama in her blood, and she's not afraid to face down anything: darkness, thunder, a stepmother that she's decided must be wicked. She invites spectacle and it clings to her, and as a queer kid, I loved that.

There can also be something queer in saying *it's not fair*, in demanding justice. Sarah sees the parts of regular life that are going to haunt her and loudly refuses them. She looks at what her life is fated to become, and she thinks: *There has to be something different.*

Choices, like wishes, can be queerly dangerous.

# 2

## *Labyrinth* and the Romance of Failure

I asked my creative writing grad students what they knew about *Labyrinth*, an eighties movie that must have been distant from their current experience. One student said they'd watched it for the first time in 2024: *I think I missed its prime by a long shot . . . I had so many unanswered questions.* Another said they hadn't seen it, but their Gen-Z sister was obsessed. A third admitted they couldn't get through it, and a fourth said they preferred *The Dark Crystal*, though they could still appreciate *Labyrinth* as *an extension of Jim Henson's brain — the darker, more experimental side of his vision.* I'm used to students critiquing the texts that I love — it's a part of teaching, and it reminds me to interrogate my own choices — but I was intrigued by how their take on *Labyrinth* seemed to replicate its own critical tradition. Even the student who loved Henson's body of work had to admit

that it wasn't their favorite. When I watch the film now, I find it to be beautiful and flawed, which are often the criteria for something becoming a cult classic. The world is haunting and impossibly detailed, the story is peculiar at times, the characters leave us with questions, the ending is both delightful and confusing. Roger Ebert, in his two-star review, famously said: *It never really comes alive.*[7] Saying that was like stabbing a puppeteer in the heart.

Was the film ahead of its time? Or was it a mess?

It's shocking to me that *Labyrinth* was pulled from theaters after only three weeks, due to poor ticket sales.[8] It's an actual miracle that I saw it on the big screen, when I was eight years old and perfectly ready for this beautiful nightmare of a film. Audiences had issues with the pacing of his earlier film, *The Dark Crystal*, but they were still prepared to see it as the innovation that it was: the first live-action puppet film, with no CGI effects, that told an epic fantasy story. Henson hired gemsmiths and armorers and architects to construct every detail of his world, and even though one critic dismissively called it *that brown movie*, it was understood to be a technical masterpiece.

The main criticism was that *The Dark Crystal* was slow-moving, somber, and lacked human actors. But even when Henson responded to this by literally casting David Bowie and making *Labyrinth* a fun and freaky musical, it still didn't

7 Ebert, "*Labyrinth*," *Rogerebert.com*, July 27, 1986.

8 This statistic is cited in Stine, "*Labyrinth* and the Dark Heart of Childhood."

work for the audience. The movie seemed to have incredible parts, but they didn't quite come together as a whole, a likely result of the fragmented script.[9] The story began as a novella written by Canadian author Dennis Lee — known for his wry fables like *Alligator Pie* — and eventually ended in the hands of *Monty Python* alum and medieval scholar Terry Jones. By the time the film premiered, Jones found the story to be unrecognizable from what he'd written, but he wasn't mad about it. He felt that Henson and his team had improved upon the original, though we have Jones to thank for the idea behind the exceedingly creepy "helping hands" scene, in which Sarah stumbles into a pit lined with green-tinged hands that can either prevent her from falling or consign her to gravity. Jim Henson and his son Brian refined these hands into a menagerie of uncanny faces, directing the actors' fingers so they formed speaking mouths that ask Sarah to choose which direction she wants to go. We'll return to this scene later.

Maurice Sendak was also a longtime collaborator with Henson, but the final version of *Labyrinth* was close enough to one of his own children's books — *Outside Over There*, about a baby abducted by goblins — that he threatened to sue Henson. Henson biographer Brian Jay Jones notes that Sendak's lawyers "advised Jim to cease production on the film,"[10] and that Henson was "stunned" by the accusation that *Labyrinth* had ripped off *Outside Over There*. It's possible that both authors

9 In his biography of Henson, Brian Jay Jones notes that writer and actress Elaine May was the final script doctor for *Labyrinth*, and that her changes helped to "humanize" Sarah's character.

10 Froud, 381.

simply tapped into deep stories with a great deal of overlap. Or perhaps Henson didn't realize how influenced he'd been by reading Sendak's earlier works to his own children. It's interesting to think of what a clearer collaboration between both storytellers might have looked like, if they'd been able to work together.

As the artist Brian Froud has pointed out, since the beginning of storytelling *goblins have always stolen babies.*[11] It's kind of their thing. Think of Christina Rossetti's "Goblin Market," that Victorian long poem where there is a constant threat of being snatched away by goblins. Nobody has ever owned this particular idea. Henson, however, was clearly influenced by Sendak's work, and the final script of *Labyrinth* was a deeply collaborative affair. Not only was it a movie written by a committee, it was also indicative of Henson's obsessive editing, since he was making changes mere days before principal filming began. Yet it's also purely Henson, in many ways. The world is painstaking and hilarious and deeply moving. There's a gentleness to the most unsettling scenes, and the ending is a joyful romp. When the trash heap in the Henson TV show *Fraggle Rock* insists that we never leave magic behind, we feel that in the credits of *Labyrinth*. There is a thematic similarity to a particular episode of *Fraggle Rock* where Wembley has to deal with the death of a friend.[12] The subject is treated with simplicity and tenderness, but child viewers aren't spared the

11 Froud, *The Goblins of Labyrinth*.

12 This episode was written by gay puppeteer Richard Hunt, who performs the dying puppet Mudwell, and it certainly feels like a story about the AIDS crisis.

idea that loved ones will vanish from their lives. Henson often used fantasy to approach realism.

And yet . . . that final scene, with Sarah dancing. Henson was even going to call some of the goblins (the ones who swap body parts during the celebratory dance) *wild things*, but eventually changed their collective name to "Fireys." The film is a delicate roadmap of flaws and missteps and failures that somehow remains delicious, like the peach that, in the middle of her adventure, sends Sarah into an enchanted dream. We taste the sweet, but there's something slightly off, a worm burrowed in the soft flesh perhaps. But maybe the worm is the point. After all, early in the film, he does invite us in for a nice cup of tea.

## FAILURE AND CREATIVITY

In *The Queer Art of Failure*, J. Halberstam asks: "What kinds of rewards can failure offer us?"[13] One of many answers to this question is: "Failure allows us to escape the punishing norms that discipline human behavior."

As I work on this chapter, I'm listening to *The Bends*, an arguably perfect album by Radiohead. But is it really perfect, or is this just my failure to move past the music of my adolescence? Every time my brain lights up when I hear a song by Garbage or the Cranberries, am I simply refusing to grow?

13 Halberstam, 3.

When I silently hum all the lyrics to "Poor Unfortunate Souls" from *The Little Mermaid*, am I embracing my queer childhood self, or failing to process all my delightfully complex trauma?

Jim Henson took failure personally. Even when *The Dark Crystal* was a technical success, he internalized the criticism. He needed to make sure that his next film wasn't too slow, too boring, too beige. When we talk about world-building in fantasy literature and film, we have to include Henson within the company of writers like Tolkien and N.K. Jemisin. He meticulously sourced wood and metal and fabric to create a multilayered world that one could literally touch. As his marriage collapsed, and his health began to decline, Henson worked without complaint to build *Labyrinth* from the ground up. He suffused it with his own philosophies on the fleeting nature of time, the darkness of childhood, and the fragility of being human. There were vicious goblins and sweet giants, mechanical monsters, seduction and memory and the trauma of fairy tales. He attended international press tours, awkward in his ill-fitting suits, trying to still his long limbs for yet another interview.

What a glorious failure *Labyrinth* was.

The reviews ranged from mediocre to bad, with a few bright spots in between. One critic said: *I just don't give a f— about the main character*. Sarah felt moody and contrary and grating to them, like Mary Lennox at the start of *The Secret Garden*, when she's still difficult and interesting. Jennifer Connelly's character falls into an impossible and eternal bind of girlhood where all of her actions are judged as failures. Sarah is too bossy, too

whiny, too critical, too childish, not sweet enough, too manipulative, too naive, kind of a bitch, not sexy enough, too nerdy but not the right kind of nerdy, not a boy. She rages at her baby brother for crying all the time, not just because he demands attention, but because he distracts her from internal world-building. She follows her instincts, even when they're wrong. She's scared. She's arrogant, at times. She loses herself in this peculiar maze of memory and desire, all while wearing blue jeans, a puffy white top, and sensible shoes.

When critics weren't complaining about Sarah, they were focused almost entirely on the odd pacing of the film, and Henson saw that as a startling and inexcusable failure. He'd given everything to ensure it wasn't slow, that it was compelling and even a little sexy, and it was rejected. Imagine if he were alive to see the fan-fueled *Labyrinth*-themed masquerade balls, still happening in 2026. Would he rethink that failure today?

*

I spent a lot of time wearing out my *Labyrinth* soundtrack cassette, while failing to connect with kids my own age. I sat on the floor of the Coles bookstore in my hometown, reading *Dragonlance* novels and wishing I could be the cranky wizard Raistlin. He'd sacrificed his health for magic, and he had golden hourglass pupils that saw the whole world dying, but he'd also gained the power to cast world-changing spells. And that was what I wanted, more than anything else. The power

of invisibility, so that I could avoid the pain of baffling social interactions.[14] The power to link words together in a coherent, unremarkable sentence, rather than standing in silence when people asked me questions. The power to not scream internally whenever I had to shower and wear clothes, because it felt like bugs crawling on my skin. When I pressed play on my Walkman — the color of a faded gray river stone — I'd hear the opening synth bars of "As the World Falls Down," and my hummingbird heart would still.

Even as Bowie sang about the world not making sense, I felt safe, because someone else understood the fractal chaos of the outside world. Adults kept looking me in the eye: *Why?* Kids looked at me with an air of suspicion, like I was some clockwork mechanism in their midst. A lot of autistic kids grew up with a burning sense of imposter syndrome, like they were cuckoos, and some folklorists have even proposed that the idea of the changeling child might have emerged as a response to autistic children. *Why are you so different from the others? What fairy realm did you come from?* In her essay "Real Autism," Sarah Kurchak talks about having nightmares as a kid, doubting her own "realness" as a person: "I was a copy that my parents had been forced to take in when the actual Sarah had died."[15] I had similar fantasies about being kidnapped from another

14 A *baffle* is also an architectural feature meant to be confusing, which makes all labyrinths baffling in a literal sense, and reminds us that the word comes from a sense of being spatially lost.

15 Kurchak, "Real Autism."

planet — so many autistic kids experienced this that it led to an online resource called *Wrong Planet*.[16]

I knew, from the top of my mullet to the tips of my high-tops, that I would follow Jareth to the heart of the labyrinth. I'd fear him, love him, and do anything he said, if he could only explain what it meant to exist in the world while we danced our way toward some kind of goblin meaning.

## GOBLIN FRUITS: REACHING FOR WHAT'S BAD

I wrote my first book at seven years old, and my dad bound it with cardboard and a piece of denim, salvaged from an old pair of jeans. I sent full manuscripts to fantasy publishers like Tor and DAW when I was 15, and nearly got scammed by a predatory literary agency because I was so desperate to see my stories in print.

I was 27 when I published my first novel, a book of modest buzz that resulted in a handful of film/TV options, and it felt like falling in love. Finally, the world made sense. I would be an *author*. I would live in New York and have sparkling lunches with my editor and teach part-time in a prestigious creative writing program. My life would be full of tours and launches, and interviews where I joked with other writers and made secretive comments about works-in-progress. No one would care about my social awkwardness, my silences, my crushing

16 This online community was started by writer/autism-activist Alex Plank (www.wrongplanet.net).

panic attacks, my undiagnosed autism, because I would actually *fit*. I'd never felt so close to achieving this, like a trembling cell about to divide into something real.

The truth is that I did have lunch with my editor, and I did sign another book contract, and I did give interviews about my weird little gay vampire book. It was a moderate success. But in spite of leading to a five-book series, it didn't "break out." My advances got lower. I was grudgingly offered another series, which flopped. Then my publisher dropped me, and like Sarah, I was lost in the maze.

It took a long time to realize that I would not be a full-time author who could live on advances and royalties alone. Very few authors can manage this, but it still felt like the kind of failure that threatened to destroy my whole consciousness. One day I was standing in Brooklyn, talking to a Hollywood director about how my first novel, *Night Child*, would be the next big procedural crime show. Then suddenly, I was marking composition essays in Regina, Saskatchewan — a place I'd never even visited before moving there — adapting to a new teaching job that would break me down in every possible way.

If my authorial optimism was a kind of original nightmare, then my academic optimism was the sinister sequel, whose run time extended well past its best-by date, long into my thirties, as I struggled to balance the demands of being a long-term author with the chaotic landscape of full-time academia. But when I was in grad school from 2001 to 2007, the optimism was like dancing in Jareth's crystal dream world. Yes, there were sinister goblins in the corners scheming to kidnap us all.

But the music. The dancing. The reckless meaning-making, and beer-fueled anxiety, and late-night conversations about words. Henson once said that life was like a labyrinth, and so is academia, except with no worm to guide us.

*

I had always been a terrible student. Not because I didn't want to learn, but because I couldn't exist in a classroom. The fluorescent lights made my teeth ache. The heat and sounds and smells made me want to crawl out of my skin. I tried to listen to the teachers, but kids were always whispering and passing notes and kicking my desk and touching me. I have a core memory of standing outside the classroom, melting down in a sweatshirt that said *Not Playing With a Full Duck*, while my sixth-grade teacher tried in vain to calm me down.

I cut class, because it was easier to read in an open field — letting the occasional raindrop splatter my copy of Diane Duane's *So You Want to Be a Wizard* — than it was to endure the sensory chaos of the school. I began to spend time with a sinister boy who also seemed like a social exile. We'd wander down to the nearby creek, where he'd talk about sex and other things I wasn't really interested in. At least he didn't ask me why I was weird. We watched *The Serpent and the Rainbow* at his house, while his mom paced like an angry, brittle ghost.

Recently, I discovered that the boy was now serving a 15-year prison sentence for murder. I remembered him as an awkward kid with a russet-colored brush cut and a high-pitched,

skittering laugh. I wonder if he remembers us, dancing around his bedroom, trying not to wake his dark outline of a father. He ended up unhoused, close to where we grew up. One day, soaring on a black cocktail of drugs, he bludgeoned a man to death with a hammer. In the mugshot, he had long braided hair, and his expression was askew, but the boy was still under there, somewhere, lost in a maze that he never had a chance of solving.

I had a goldfish; he had a dog that barked violently. I have a Ph.D.; he's in prison. But for an odd moment, we were so close, walking along the edge of the dirty brown slough, our own version of *Labyrinth*'s Bog of Eternal Stench. Both of us unable, for our own reasons, to tolerate what the world was trying to make of us.

## THE ART OF FAILING

As an English instructor who teaches first-year composition classes, I think a lot about failure. My colleague Medrie Purdham has said that one of her primary goals in teaching a first-year academic writing class — which often includes a significant population of international students who struggle with English — is to keep students from harm. There are so many ways to accidentally or purposefully fail in a class like this. A student might fail to properly attribute a source, or simply forget to place a line of text in quotation marks. They might use an online tool that forms the structure of their essay,

without actually doing the work required to properly format the assignment. They might include AI-generated information, perhaps by accident, perhaps on purpose with the hope that it will go unnoticed. They could even write a thoughtful, engaging paper, and then submit a bibliography full of gaps that necessitates a discussion of academic misconduct. There are so many mistakes that students can and will make at this level, and some of them have far-reaching consequences, especially for students whose financial and geographic security depends upon maintaining a certain grade. In her conference paper "Machine Learning and Assessment Practice," Brenna Clarke Gray notes that generative AI has created "a moment for reassessing assessment and for considering how we can centre process, and not only the final product."[17] This means paying more attention to how students work through the writing process, and how they often fail at key moments, just as we all fail daily and radically at being "proper" humans.

*Labyrinth* is a movie about failure. Sarah fails to be a dutiful daughter, a good sister, a social being with friends and evening plans. Instead, she practices dramatic monologues in the park with her dog and wishes that her annoying baby brother would literally be kidnapped by monsters. But the film's most fascinating monster — the Goblin King — is also a critical failure. He rules over a dingy, crumbling kingdom and spends most of his time looking bored and petulant in a goblin-infested throne room. He also fails to capture Sarah because,

17 Clarke Gray, "On Machine Learning and Academic Learning."

as the film reminds us, he never had any *real* power over her to begin with. What kind of villain is that?

Sarah's companions are an awkward band of monstrous misfits. Ludo, a giant hairy beast, almost completely fails to be frightening. Instead, he speaks in a tender grumble, delighted that Sarah might be his first real friend. Sir Didymus, the pint-sized knight, fails to uphold the protocols of chivalry because he can't protect Sarah. And Hoggle, Sarah's unreliable guide through the labyrinth, is the biggest failure of all.[18] He sprays fairies with pesticide, steals trinkets, lies, cheats, and eventually betrays Sarah to the Goblin King. He's a self-proclaimed coward, and his deception nearly traps Sarah within a nightmarish dream vision, where she must dance at a masquerade forever. Nobody comes to save her, least of all her heroic companions. In spite of the celebrated power of friendship, Sarah is ultimately alone.

When Jim Henson and artist Brian Froud were coming up with ideas for the story, Froud suggested that a maze "would make a really good metaphor for the soul's journey." But how do you turn that into a marketable movie for children? And is *Labyrinth* a kids' movie anyway? Henson was always adamant that his puppetry was for adults as well and that he wasn't actually a children's entertainer. But the character of the Goblin King was also originally supposed to be a singing and

18 Hoggle was notoriously difficult to operate. Brian Henson served as his voice, but his body movements were controlled by actress Shari Weiser, and there were other puppeteers who controlled his face. Aside from Humongous, he was the most complex puppet in the film, which is such an interesting choice, given that he was both an unpopular and untrustworthy character.

dancing puppet. Imagine a film whose dark, seductive core was not David Bowie, but rather, a malicious Muppet.

The more one delves into the history of this film and its production, the more it feels like Henson was never truly certain how to execute the story. He understood its deep themes — fragility, injustice, the horrors of childhood, and the relentless march of time — but even after a team of writers edited the script 25 times, it never felt complete. Was that Henson's failure to produce something that could be properly visualized within a commercial film? Or was it the constant interference of a capitalist film industry, which was always trying to flatten Henson's rich ideas? He celebrated the film's premiere by hosting an Elizabethan masquerade, where he could ghost through the crowd in a disguise. And perhaps that was a kind of failure as well: Henson the shrewd businessman trying to dance with Henson the shy introvert.

*Labyrinth* was basically his heart on a platter, and when someone (in this case, the audience) rejects your innermost core, how can you ever recover?

In their book *Cruel Optimism*, Lauren Berlant describes the ways in which we strive for things — particularly goals and fantasies of living — that actually hurt us.

> A relation of cruel optimism exists when something you desire is actually an obstacle to your flourishing. It might involve food, or a kind of love; it might be a fantasy of the good life, or a political project. It might rest

> on something simpler, too, like a new habit that promises to induce in you an improved way of being.[19]

We often want things that are harmful, but this goes deeper than simply being attached to a vice, like alcohol or smoking. We can attach love, value, even a sense of completion, to things that don't love us back. Things that, in the end, may destroy us, in spite of how much we want and need them. Hence, the heartbreak.

It's one thing to know that something is poisonous. It's another to slowly realize, over the course of your life, that the dream or experience you've attached your personhood to might be holding you back in painful ways. That the life you trusted will betray you, like a goblin in a labyrinth. There are things that we spend our whole lives trying to grasp, and even when we get our hands around them, we discover how impossible it is to maintain that posture of reaching. We break ourselves, again and again, in the grasping.

*

In the second season of *Fleabag*, Phoebe Waller-Bridge's character begs the hot priest to simply tell her what to do:

> I want someone to tell me what to wear in the morning . . . what to like, what to hate, what to rage about . . . I

19 Berlant, 1.

just want someone to tell me how to live my life, Father, because so far I think I've been getting it wrong.[20]

The Goblin King's spell is the same, ultimately, as what Fleabag asks for: to live under a force that will structure your life. To serve something mysterious and let that power make all your decisions for you. As a tired adult in their forties, I have to say, this offer is tempting. Of course I'd crawl under Jareth's cloak. If you asked me today, I'd flee underground to the Goblin City, where I'd never have to check my email again. Sarah isn't scared. In fact, she defies Jareth in the final moment. Maybe Jareth's promise to remove her character from the hell of public teen girlhood wasn't actually that tempting.

But I choose goblin every time.

*Labyrinth* offers us a kind of grace, because it normalizes the experience of failure. Sarah makes bad choices, and then she makes good ones, and there are still a few more bad ones mixed in. We forgive her for giving her baby brother to the Goblin King, because she's a child herself, still trying to figure out how to move through the world. In fact, at every crucial moment in the film, she's uncertain, all the way to end. When she finally finds Toby and leaps toward him as Jareth's castle falls apart, she's leaping into the unknown. Henson's former assistant, Mira Velimirovic, describes the plot of *Labyrinth* as the act of growing up: "Adolescence is a labyrinth that we all move through."[21]

---

20 Waller-Bridge, *Fleabag*, 2.04, March 25, 2019.

21 *Labyrinth*, Blu-ray featurette, 2009.

Hoggle betrays Sarah out of fear. Ludo finds himself hanging upside down, helpless. Even Sarah's stepmother can't figure out how to claim a place in her new life: "She treats me like a wicked stepmother from a fairy tale, no matter what I do." The characters in the film are so often falling apart, falling down, yelling or crying in frustration, because that's what it feels like to move through the corridors of adolescence toward an unknown adulthood.

Yes, a tiny goblin might be erasing your lipstick marks on the stones, scrubbing away your path home as you go. And a monster likely awaits you at the heart of things, preparing to fascinate you and break you down all at the same time. But then a nice beast just might grab your hand, pulling you along in its warm grasp before you can think twice and look back.

# 3

## Goblin Mode and Liberation

Goblins have never been especially popular within the epic fantasy tradition. They tend to slink around in the shadows, worrying at the edges of role-playing games or medievalist stories. Though George MacDonald's *The Princess and the Goblin* remains a children's classic, and a foundational Victorian fantasy text, it's never achieved the popularity of *Alice in Wonderland* or *The Hobbit*. Goblins do appear in Tolkien's famous children's novel, but mostly as a racist "tribe" living under the Misty Mountains. They're described as gluttonous and cruel, even though they're never considered serious villains.

The goblinish prototype is a mischievous household spirit. Sometimes they wear red caps, sometimes they throw furniture around like a poltergeist, but in general, they lack the ferocity of a traditional monster. If you've ever played an action

role-playing game, goblins are often the first creatures you'll have to fight in order to advance to a higher level of experience. I remember in the nineties, at the height of the *Magic: The Gathering* craze, when a stack of goblin cards was described as a *weenie deck*. In packs, they were considered mildly annoying, but who cared about a lone goblin? Who would agree to playing an entire campaign as a goblin, with mismatched armor and no discernible skills? They were always considered an initial obstacle, rather than a force to be respected, or even intrigued by. They were the footnotes and foot soldiers of the genre's monstrous underside. We hardly know anything about them.

## GOBLIN ORIGINS

Nobody can quite agree on where the word *goblin* comes from, or what a goblin is, for that matter. In his multi-volume *Teutonic Mythology*, Jacob Grimm — that famous compiler of dark stories — traces the word back to the German *kobold*. This, in turn, goes back to the Latin *cobalus*, which can be either a mischievous spirit or the type of household god that the ancient Romans honored with domestic altars. Not an unwanted guest, precisely, but something very much alive in the foundations of your home. Treat them well, pay them the right amount of attention, and they'll ensure the integrity of the house. Scorn them, and they'll tear apart everything you know or lead you into an inescapable forest. The queer poet Cavafy wrote about the lares, the Roman household gods,

"trembling" at the arrival of true divinity.[22] Perhaps, as queer people, we sometimes feel like those godlings: tolerated for the most part, but always wary of receiving the wrong kind of attention from the more powerful, glamorous gods.

I used to play a game called *Hero's Quest* (later renamed *Quest for Glory*, though that seemed inaccurate, since the series was satirical). This was the late eighties, when adventure games had made the leap from pure text to 16-color graphics, but they still felt more like *Choose Your Own Adventure* novels. In *Hero's Quest*, your character has recently graduated from a heroic correspondence school, and your quest is to save the quirky village of Spielburg from an unnamed evil. Games like this had a text box interface, called a parser, where you'd input commands. *Climb tree. Open chest. Run.* You built up skills through repetitive actions, and I loved the soothing process of typing the same command, over and over. I wanted a text parser for reality, which would allow me to communicate properly. I'd feed it commands like *understand facial expression* or *translate sarcasm*, and then I could level up socially.

One of the more fascinating in-game monsters was a kobold, who lived in a cave. I loved this point in the game, because the cave was painted in cool purples and blues, like an underwater sanctuary. The kobold was a wizened little nut-brown man, guarding a chest. I would have been happy in the kobold's cave, whose entrance was guarded by a bear. We could all hibernate.

22 Cavafy, "The Footsteps," *Knopf.*

One of the most delightful connections in Grimm's *Teutonic Mythology* is the idea that kobolds might be related to nutcrackers. He points out that the earliest nutcrackers, with their crude wooden bodies, were probably meant to resemble goblins. That makes them, I have to believe, the household gods of Christmas, protecting the holiday from thieves in the night by their perch beside the holiday nut bowl. My boyfriend and I have a tradition of purchasing a small live tree, which fits perfectly near our bear-themed nativity set. The tree is decorated with glitter-bright nutcrackers, and I think of them as queer little kobolds, exchanging secrets with the cat while we sleep.

## GOBLIN FREEDOMS

The plot of *Labyrinth* emerged as Jim Henson was driving in a limo with Brian and Wendy Froud, a moment that was a study in contrasts for Henson, once the quiet kid from Mississippi, now being routinely ferried across vast cities in a limousine. Froud met Wendy on the set of *The Dark Crystal*, and their son Toby would play the eponymous baby in *Labyrinth*. The three adults were bound together, as if by magic.

Henson originally wanted the follow-up to *The Dark Crystal* to focus on colorful flying gods, which he'd learned about through his daughter Lisa's undergraduate work in mythology. Froud said he didn't know much about the subject: *But I* do *know*

*about goblins.*[23] It was a funny thing to claim — an expertise in those queer little things that nobody could quite define, the spirits who kept our homes in working order.

In this and other ways, goblins share our human nature more than other monsters. They can be big or small, helpful or wicked. They can turn on you, as humans do, as feral cats will bite the hand they mistrust. The goblinish Puck deceives the lovers in *A Midsummer Night's Dream*, and while he doesn't necessarily mean them harm, he disrupts their lives and exposes them to the danger of the fairy world. In *Labyrinth*, Hoggle offers Sarah a poisoned peach — he does it out of fear, but his actions still remove her sense of agency by trapping her in a dream world. Goblins, like humans, make poor decisions, not always out of malice. Sometimes they're fumbling through a difficult world, just like us.

Henson chose Bowie to portray the Goblin King because he wanted an actor that could combine fantasy and reality. The audience wouldn't forget the glittery context of Bowie's alt-music persona, but he was also mutable, called upon to constantly shift from one form to another: a king, a crystal, a blind old goblin, a magnificent swan. Froud describes him as "part rockstar, part dangerous goblin . . . he is a knight from Grimm's fairy tales, with the worms of death eating through his armor." Perhaps the friendly worm served as a reminder of this. After all, someone needed to devour the souls lost in

23 Jones, *Jim Henson: The Biography*, 355.

the labyrinth. Not even Jareth was immune to the decay at the heart of his weird musical kingdom.

The most well-known literary goblins come from Christina Rossetti's poem "Goblin Market." Two sisters battle the seductive power of goblins, who offer them a selection of distressingly sexy fruit. "Leering at each other / brother with queer brother." Arthur Rackham's illustrations give the goblins a sly, cat-like mood. Laura is obsessed with all this queer juice, but can't pay for it, and soon begins to waste away. Lizzie faces down the goblins, just as Sarah faces down the unsettling Fireys, and steals some fruit pulp to give to her sister. Laura sucks the juice from Lizzie's flesh, and nearly becomes a goblin herself, but by morning, she's an ordinary girl again. The word *queer* surfaces multiple times within the poem, and, like *goblin*, it's a term with a twisting etymology. Not always a negative word, it's often meant as different or strange. As a homophobic insult, it crystallized the sense of something unnatural, aberrant. But its older meaning was something close to *slantwise*, something a bit crooked, a bit unexpected, hovering at the corner of your vision, like the shifting Escher-style staircases in *Labyrinth*. When Sarah eats the poison peach — created by Jareth to trap her within her own dreams — Henson is surely thinking of "Goblin Market" and its wild fruit.

Goblins can give you almost anything, but the price is always exorbitant. Sarah nearly wastes away, like Laura, in a sinister masquerade, surrounded by goblin aristocrats, in a pantomime of one of her heart's greatest desires. In fact, the ball's details — from the color of her white dress to the

music — is taken from a music box in her real-life bedroom. The clock is always ticking, always counting the time you have left to complete your life's tasks (or save your baby brother), but if you dance forever — or work forever — you should be able to make your dreams come true.

In this way, Henson conveys the artist in all of us, racing against time and the hostile landscape of our own goblin cities, our untrustworthy and shifting bodies. But if we can just keep dancing, or writing, nothing bad will happen. Keep moving or imagining or creating until you force your life into submission. How many times have I turned to the order of writing when my life was in flames?

## GOBLINS AND TRANSFORMATION

In her self-care book *Goblin Mode*, McKayla Coyle asserts that "goblins know that every pile of clutter has a warm, dark, cozy center . . . [Being] a goblin is all about escaping the claws of capitalism (to the extent that anyone can)."[24] The aesthetic of the goblins in *Labyrinth* is definitely what Coyle would call "goblincore." The goblin soldiers wear mismatched pieces of armor and carry broken swords. An old, "wise" goblin, who Sarah meets early on in the film, wears another birdlike goblin as a hat. When the bearded goblin tries to offer nonsensical advice like "the way forward is sometimes the way back," their

24 Coyle, chap. 4, ebook.

sarcastic hat-goblin delivers the memeable line: "It's so stimulating being your head."

The Firey goblins wear fur instead of clothes and happily deconstruct their own bodies, tossing limbs and heads at Sarah as she tries to escape their ominous "chill" dance (isn't it the ultimate relaxation when our bodies finally fall apart?). The Goblin King wears flowing cloaks, ruffles, lace, and jewelry that might have come from Etsy. He's unquestionably at home in his own labyrinth, and his fabulous outfits have a frayed quality to them as well — everything in his world is always softly disintegrating, like the dark, cozy center of an anxious brain. While many villains of eighties cinema wear suits, Jareth lounges in his slightly inappropriate leggings. He stims with his crystals and sometimes leaves a conversation by turning into an owl. As a villain — if that's actually what he is — he seems indisputably comfortable. Cozy, even.

*

Jareth's body is tricky. He's seductive not only through Bowie's undeniable beauty, but because he's never just one thing. *Just fear me*, he urges Sarah, *love me*. In the final scene of the broken castle, with time itself in disarray, he shimmers in his downy owl cloak. He says that he's re-altered time *for* Sarah, but actually, it's to keep her from saving Toby. I watched this scene over and over as a child, until I could draw each feather from memory.

We understand in this moment what Froud was saying about Jareth's dangerous hybridity. He was always "part dangerous

goblin,"[25] never fully human. But the reverse is also true of Sarah, who faces him down, just as Lizzie faced down the goblins to rescue her sister in "Goblin Market." Sarah is more than a teenage girl, or perhaps Henson's message is that all teenage girls are more than they seem. Her room is a collection of jewels and memories and fragments of childhood that she stubbornly, rightly refuses to give up.

Henson and Froud both engineered the Goblin King as a symbol of Sarah's unconscious desires, her daydreams and nightmares. But it's facile to say that Sarah merely realizes that Jareth lives inside of her, that she has to perform some kind of psychic integration, and then she can finally grow up.

That's simply not what happens in film or in life.

*

Like Sarah, Henson was torn between the childish image of puppetry and its potential for sophisticated, adult storytelling. He went on a grand tour of Italy to research commedia dell'arte, which included traditions going back to Ancient Greece. We've always used puppets and mannequins and shadows to tell human stories. Henson wanted to tell those very same stories, and he always resisted being corralled as a child's performer. But he was also passionately interested in the experience of childhood, and much of his finest art builds a bridge between children and adults.

25 Froud, *The Goblins of Labyrinth*, 141.

The richest idea in Henson's work is *radical play*: the idea of harnessing childhood delights and emotions and carrying them into the adult world. The author Madeleine L'Engle famously said that if a story was too complex for adults, you should tell it to children. All of us, regardless of age, are wandering through the same forests and labyrinths, whether led there by tricky kobolds or by our own complex decisions. We're all a little lost, and even when we find a helpful worm to guide us, they'll likely send us in the wrong direction. As the old goblin tells Sarah, *the way forward is sometimes the way back*. By the end of the film, Sarah realizes that Jareth is powerless, but the key to her emancipation is more than that one revelation. She also refuses to accept the end of childhood's peculiar power, and so she carries that spell into her own adolescence. She holds a wild dance in her bedroom, where she can dance with — or be — any goblin she chooses.

I've always been in love with shape-shifters. The sorceress from *Masters of the Universe*, who could become a falcon at will. Odo from *Deep Space Nine*, who once surrendered to a puddle of starlit goo, sighing in relief as he dissolved in a Betazoid's purse. The ability to vanish into a sea of light, a flurry of feathers. I desired Bowie in a straightforward gay way, but also in a queer way that had more to do with gender than sexuality. I wanted to steal his feather cloak and slip into the form of an owl. I wanted to pull off my own limbs and become flame, like the medieval Saint Christina the Astonishing, who was said to have transmuted herself to a molten ball. Why couldn't I just be the wind, or Godzilla, or some secret alchemical mutation?

Perhaps what I really wanted to be was a goblin, sly and transformative and agender. I'd argue that Sarah wanted the same thing. She wasn't calling boys with feathered hair on a Saturday night, boys who would ultimately disappoint her. Instead, she's dancing with the beautiful monsters of her childhood, all the best and worst parts of herself. She's been them all, and so have we, in our desires, our explorations of gender, the clothes we've chosen to walk through the world in. Commenting on the recent explosion of laws meant to erase trans people from public existence and strip reproductive freedoms, Judith Butler asks: "Can we even *say* how many contemporary fears gather at the site of gender?"[26] Henson's work offers a resistance to the genocidal policies that target gender-diverse individuals. The sense of play in his work extends to all forms of gender transformation and transition. Gender is a labyrinth, and we all deserve the pleasure of being lost in it, only to find ourselves in the most surprising corners.

*

Reviewers generally enjoyed the goblins in *Labyrinth*, praising Henson's workshop for its technical marvels. What they didn't like was Jennifer Connelly's performance as Sarah. Gene Siskel cruelly called her "forgettable."[27] Nina Darnton, while drawing links to Sendak and the darker fables of E.T.A. Hoffmann,

26 Butler, *Who's Afraid of Gender?*, 11.

27 Siskel, "Jim Henson's Wizardry Lost in *Labyrinth*," 21.

described Connelly's performance as "disappointing . . . she looks right, but she lacks conviction and seems to be reading rehearsed lines that are recited without belief in her goal or real need to accomplish it."[28] Imagine telling a 15-year-old actress that her performance as one of only two human characters in a film was like a blank page. *Sorry, looks like you can't even play yourself.* Critics responded to a story about the perils of girlhood, and the impossibilities of growing up, by focusing on the uneven performance of its teen lead. As Connelly/Sarah hesitated between childhood and adolescence, refusing to give up her goblin dreams and the darker powers of the labyrinth itself, she couldn't even escape the eye of critics.

Oddly enough, reviewers never compared Sarah to other teen actresses that were popular in eighties films, like Molly Ringwald or Ally Sheedy. It was as if they didn't know who they were looking at. Was she playing an ordinary girl, or a princess, or a hero? I think it's worth mentioning again that Connelly spends most of the film wearing an old pair of blue jeans and sensible shoes. In spite of her unsettling chemistry with the (immortal?) Goblin King, she's never clearly placed before the male gaze. Like Laura Dern's Ellie Sattler in the later film *Jurassic Park*, she's too busy *solving problems*. I wonder if that was the issue. Not Connelly's subtle line readings, but Henson's unwillingness to make her an object. Instead, her sexuality remains subterranean, dreamlike, as complex as the labyrinth itself.

---

28 Darnton, "Jim Henson's *Labyrinth*."

When Sarah first considers summoning the Goblin King, the film cuts away to a dark space, where goblins are piled in what I can only describe as a fur-cuddle. One wears a horned helmet; another has wild gray hair; another resembles a kind of demon Chihuahua. They're all squeezed together in the dark, but the scene isn't really ominous, because the demons are gripped by the pleasure of anticipation. "She's going to *say* it," they whisper in delight. The "right words" that will summon Jareth and seal the fate of Sarah's baby brother. The goblins murmur and giggle and shift in the confines of their world. They're all touching, inseparable from each other, a queer goblin collective. They aren't gendered in any clear way. Some of their voices are high, some low, some scratchy, some annoyed. The goblins are just . . . goblins. And isn't that a valid gender?

When I wear my decomposing, ten-year-old Adidas shorts and my ragged *Trans Joy is Resistance* tank top that I cut myself in a fit of stoned creativity,[29] I feel like more of a goblin than a tenured professor. When I take a hit of my vape-pen while listening to the Indigo Girls, covered in a veil of Crispy Minis dust, texting all of my friends to see if they're okay, I'm deep in my goblincore era. This is who I really am. Not the fun creative writing prof who cracks jokes at department meetings. I'm an awkward, grimy, unkempt goblin who wishes they could stop showering and live under a blanket with a pile of weird Old English riddles. *Labyrinth* offers us not only an

29 This tank top is designed by trans artist Mars Wright — support trans artists!

alternative to teen romance (try a goblin polycule instead!), but also a solution to the feeling that we'll never measure up to the expectations of capitalist society. Be a goblin. Say your right words. Find yourself in the fire and grime. Don't settle for the tidy Hobbit Hole (though Hobbit Hole does sound like it could be a goblin sex club).

Put on your horns. Let your hair grow wild. Burrow down deep, into the underground.

## QUEER LITTLE GOBLINS

When I moved to Regina, I was surprised that it had a gay bar. Though it was the provincial capital, it still felt too small to support that kind of queer space. Seeing the flash of the rainbow sign as I drove down Broad Street was a startling moment. Over time, I discovered that the GLCR Club (Gay and Lesbian Community of Regina) was a multipurpose space that acted as a hub for the entire community. The bar had existed in some form since the early eighties, and before that, queer and trans folks would gather at a seventies molly house on Smith Street — close to where I live now. The GLCR hosts everything from innovative drag shows to AIDS fundraisers to Christmas dinners for community members who no longer have access to family during the holidays. They battled continually with the city to maintain a licensed, covered patio in the back of the bar, so that patrons could stay safe and avoid street harassment. When you're queer in a small town, you spend a

lot of time in multipurpose spaces, trying to find community. Or you yell at town hall meetings, where various administrative figures describe you as marginalized and insignificant at best, perverts and pedophiles at worst.

Writer and activist Kai Cheng Thom notes that she's "not a big believer in justice . . . it can be frustrating and elusive." For the last several years, my community has been fighting against legislation that targets trans youth in Saskatchewan by outing them at school and refusing them access to pronouns. As the provincial government attempts to squeeze us into non-existence, I think about the impossibility of justice. But Thom believes in and advocates for love: "[Love] that is radical, love that digs deep . . . love for the community that has failed us all."[30] Communities aren't perfect, and we often have to forgive them their failures. As neo-fascism reaches a fever pitch, it becomes all the more important to understand allyship as an uneasy pact. Almost like a fairy contract. We might not love all of our allies, but we can still support them on the battlefield in the Goblin City.

My friend Laura Jane was recently walking home from the downtown mall, when a group of teens began calling her transphobic slurs. At first, she tried to become invisible, to let the moment pass. But then, in a moment of defiance, she turned around and yelled: *Boo!*

The teens drew back, startled. Did they see themselves, for the first time? Did they see her as the woman she was,

30 Thom, *I Hope We Choose Love*, 91.

or some enchantress, like Morgan le Fay, who would curse them with beautiful knowledge? I can't see their faces, but I can see hers. A face beautifully changed, since we first met, to the woman that she's always been.

## THE PLEASURES OF GOBLINHOOD

As we've learned from Coyle's *Goblin Mode*, being a goblin can mean resisting the rhythms of capitalism. Sleep in. Don't shower. Mummify yourself in crumbs. Call in goblin to work. My partner and I often joke about being *just a little guy*. We're adults with a car and a mortgage and a cat with grain allergies, so we have to buy her expensive food. But how much space really separates us from our childhood bedrooms? If people squint, they'll be able to see the goblin under our clothes, the little guy who just wants to party underground.

I think about the goblin in the "Magic Dance" scene, who just wants to crouch beneath a giant goblin keg, drinking goblin beer. There are chickens in Jareth's throne room. A baby leaps and laughs. Everything is joyful chaos, and Bowie sings about not being able to decide on the correct spell. Isn't that our daily experience? Figuring out the spell that we need to get through whatever social gauntlet life throws at us? The right nail shade, the right cardigan, the right shoes and earrings: all of these can be spells. But deep down, wouldn't it be simpler to just drink goblin beer on the filthy floor, with the demon

chickens? Okay, they're probably just regular chickens. But maybe they've become demonic by association.

*Labyrinth* teaches us that being a goblin isn't just about dancing or flapping or turning into a mildly pervy ball of flame and feathers. It's about saying no to the impossible pace of capitalist life, of the traditional markers of adolescence and adulthood. It's about refusal. And perhaps more importantly, it's about listening to your goblin body, and letting it take you where it wants to go. Another eighties icon, David Byrne of Talking Heads, tells us to stop making sense. That's a goblin anthem. Let your body stop making sense. Let it crumble and sprout hairs and develop a scent like your childhood carpet. Goblin your way into an awkward, beautiful dance of resistance. Or just sink underground. There's a party there, and nobody cares what you're wearing. Only what you are or what you can become.

# 4

## Ways of Being Green

*Labyrinth* has a distinct color palette: gold, white, rust, sandstone, and the distinct red-and-white stripes of Toby's pajamas (a custom-made outfit, like everything in the film). The goblins are a shifting mass of brown and earth tones, which you'd expect from creatures who cling to sunless spots in the labyrinth. There's always something earth-bound to them, as if they've emerged from a cave or a junkyard. Henson's world has a deeply weathered quality, and we get the sense that Jareth has been ruling over this place for centuries, like a petulant landlord, just watching it fall apart. Imagine all that infrastructure, rusting and crumbling. The goblins can only manage so much upkeep without any guidance. When Sarah and Hoggle push on a wall to escape the "cleaners" — a murderous machine piloted by multiple goblins — the wall simply gives way.

Everything is in a state of glorious disrepair, which you don't expect in a fantasy world. It's like Sarah's dreams and imagined playworlds, the inspirations for this entire place, are already oxidized. And while green might not seem central to the film's color story, it pops up in surprising places. Green, as we know, was a color close to Jim Henson's heart, though Kermit actually began as a beloved scrap of his mother's blue coat.

Is it silly to say that green is my favorite color? In spite of my inevitable arc as a queer person toward cosmic theories like astrology and tarot, it still seems odd to admit having a relationship with a color. But I also continually apologize to inanimate objects for running into them — *sorry, table leg* — so maybe it's just habit. As a teenager, I wore nothing but gray, because I wanted to disappear. But as a child of the eighties, I also had a neon color scheme. The eighties were in perfect synthesis with a film like *Labyrinth*, because everyone's house or apartment was a pile of brown carpet, but the characters inside wore bright green fanny packs and geometric designs. We were trying to stand out against all of that umber.

I've tried to dress like David from *Schitt's Creek*, in a collection of fashion-forward, bichromatic outfits. But as I've grown older and become more comfortable with my body — and whatever my gender is — I crave color: bright orange, green, and purple, graphic t-shirts, neon pink. The worm's shock of blue hair in *Labyrinth* reminds us that colors still dazzle in this crumbling world. Sarah never seems comfortable in her white gown when she is trapped in the masquerade ball — she literally breaks out of that fantasy. What she wants

is that riot of color in her bedroom, the dance of goblins all around.

Sometimes, when I wear a bright outfit to a department meeting, I feel self-conscious. *Does this* Buffy the Vampire Slayer *shirt make me look childish?* Henson's work is always addressing the false dichotomy and separation of child/adult. "It's all about transition," he says, speaking of both adolescence and the film itself.[31] When Sarah is challenged to give up her childhood, she refuses. Why shouldn't we?

Autistic people — women, in particular — can be stereotyped as childish. We might love anime and stuffed animals, be drawn to bright colors, or enjoy children's literature. We might be asexual and aromantic, which is often equated with a kind of "innocence," because sexual relationships are considered a benchmark of adulthood. In the streaming series *Heartstopper*, based on the graphic novel of the same name, the character Isaac complains that all of his friends are in couples. "It makes me feel awful, because it's not something I want for myself."[32] He's always got his head in a book, while his friends are kissing and whispering. My office is full of stuffed animals — including Fraggles — and my partner has a shelf for his Hot Wheels. Is this "childish"? We never say "adultish" to mean "too adult," but it feels like a valid comparison. Part of Sarah's journey through the labyrinth involves realizing that life isn't a maze to be solved, but an experience to be had,

31 *Labyrinth* Blu-ray featurette.

32 Oseman, *Heartstopper*, 3.03.

in countless ways. If my partner falls in love with someone else, that doesn't have to be an end. Just an unexpected turn, like the door in the oubliette behind which Sarah finds herself trapped, and that Hoggle turns upside down in order to save her. He throws it open, and light floods the chamber: she must recalibrate and start again. A true unexpected turn.

## *LABYRINTH* AND CHIVALRY

*Sir Gawain and the Green Knight* is another enigmatic fantasy story that involves the pain of adolescence. Gawain is the youngest of King Arthur's knights, and also the king's nephew, so he's under pressure to be a *good* knight. During the Christmas feast, a giant green knight appears and stirs up shit. He calls the knights of Camelot "beardless boys," and challenges the king to combat. Gawain intercedes, and the knight offers him a strange bargain, similar to the Goblin King's: *Deal me a blow with my own axe, and a year from now, I'll return the blow*. Gawain is like Sarah when she crows: "I think I'm getting smarter! It's a piece of cake!" He uses the knight's giant axe to chop off his head. Blood fountains up, and aristocrats scream. Then the knight calmly puts his head back on and says: *See you in a year*. Gawain is obviously terrified. But he has no choice — chivalry, like adulthood, demands his compliance.

He experiences his own labyrinth while searching for the green knight's castle in an attempt to uphold his agreement,

and it turns out to be yet another kind of maze: a storybook castle made of impossible angles and confectionary towers. The host of the castle is a jolly figure, much like Jareth, who enters into yet another bargain with the young knight: *Anything I win in the hunt, I'll give to you; anything you win in my castle, you'll give to me.* We shouldn't enter into confounding deals with strange entities. But do we ever read the fine print? No, we reach for that queer goblin fruit instead, because we can't help ourselves.

It turns out that the host's wife is very interested in Gawain. When the lady kisses Gawain, he has to "give" the kiss back to the host. This results in what medievalists have called the "game of kisses," which is a pretty gay literary device for a fourteenth-century Middle English poem. When Gawain first kisses the host, it feels more polite — tit for tat, as it were (buss for buss?). But the kisses grow more passionate as time wears on, until their final kiss is described as "savory."

Just as Sarah faces down Jareth at the end of *Labyrinth*, Gawain has to eventually face down the terrifying green knight. In David Lowery's wonderfully dark film adaptation of the poem, Dev Patel as Gawain slowly becomes possessed by the spirit of the green knight. But before he diminishes into a crumbling monarch, Patel's version of Gawain meets the host on horseback in a forest clearing. The host touches Gawain's cheek. "There *is* something," he says, though we're not sure what *something* is. "And I think . . . I can take it." Then he kisses Gawain, softly but firmly. What is he taking? What is the game all about? Gawain and Sarah both wander through a

world of shadow and reflection, never sure of what they truly want from their different mazes.

*

One of the most lovable characters in *Labyrinth* is Sir Didymus, a knight who guards the bridge that leads to the Bog of Eternal Stench. In the featurette to the film's DVD release, Brian Froud talks about how Sir Didymus began as a doodle in the margins: "Like a lot of my work, he was neither one thing nor another . . . part-terrier, part-squirrel."[33] Terry Jones loved this image of a ridiculous knight. He transformed the character into an almost dangerously loyal guardian, whose steed happened to be a miniature version of Sarah's dog, Merlin. You can buy a plush version of the dog-knight on Etsy, and don't think I haven't almost clicked on "purchase" after drinking one sour too many. There's a scene where Sir Didymus hangs from one of Ludo's long orange locks, a bit like a disgruntled lodger, though not as scary. We're meant to see them as a funny exercise in scale: big monster, little knight. But there's also a more subtle conversation going on that encompasses big ideas like chivalry, ethics, and the rules that we often ascribe to genres like fairy tales — rules that can be bent or broken.

Like Sir Gawain, Sir Didymus attempts to follow the rules of chivalry. He wants, more than anything else, to be a good knight. Geoffrey Chaucer's *The Canterbury Tales* also focuses

33 *Labyrinth* Blu-ray, Froud commentary.

on grand concepts like chivalry, justice, and love. The narrator of the tales, often considered a self-insert for Chaucer himself, is an introvert. He's shy, awkward, and makes terrible eye contact (same). When he finally steps into the spotlight to share a tale with the other pilgrims, his story is about a little toy knight who rides his tiny steed through the tall grass. There's no doubt that Terry Jones, a medievalist himself — who's written a book on Chaucer — was thinking about this wee chivalric parody when he fleshed out the character of Sir Didymus. In the *The Canterbury Tales*, everyone complains about the narrator's tale. Their host, who runs the tavern where the wannabe pilgrims trade stories, proclaims it to be *not worth a turd*. But in *Labyrinth*, the little knight gets his moment, and it's hard not to enjoy watching this super-charged squirrel dart across the screen.

A bit like Henson himself, Sir Didymus is keenly concerned with justice and fairness. In spite of his size, he guards the bridge with ferocity, because he's convinced that it's a noble task. Though he courteously addresses Sarah as "my lady," it's clear that he has no intention of letting her pass. A knight stays on-mission. But when Sarah finally inquires what his mission actually is, the whole project turns out to be circular. He guards the bridge because he's always guarded the bridge, and none shall pass without his permission. By this point, Sarah has come to realize that solving the labyrinth involves taking apart difficult puzzles, all of which relate to the experience of being human. Instead of trying to overpower this unpredictable fuzz-knight, she asks him the most logical question that

she can think of: *Can we have your permission?* Sir Didymus is confused by this. He frowns in thought for a bit and replies, with a fair amount of uncertainty: *Yes?* It's silly and very Monty Python–esque, with a callback to the bridge-guarding wizard in *Holy Grail.* But it's also a moment about critical thinking. Sarah treats him like a person, rather than a toy, and he consequently realizes that knights can think for themselves.

Both *Labyrinth* and *Sir Gawain and the Green Knight* are texts that intimately understand the feeling of failure. Sarah fails, in so many ways, to exist as a normative teenage girl in the Reagan Eighties. The film failed to be a box-office success, and Henson considered it to be one of his most painful failures as an artist, because he invested so much personally in the story's production. Gawain fails to abide by the rules of chivalry, even as the poem exposes these rules to be impossible. A knight, the poem says, is inhuman. They're an assemblage of person, horse, blade, honor, and if you remove one of those elements or change their conditions even slightly, they dissolve. Gawain can't accept the green knight's invitation to live in his castle. He has to return to Camelot, because Arthur loves a good story, and this story can't fully be real until he delivers it to a captive audience. The court will laugh at him, indulgently. Nobles will *ooh* and *ahh* over the scar on his neck, the green knight's final kiss.

But his experience is what's important, especially the moment when Gawain realizes that chivalry is a failed project, and you can be fair without having to follow a bunch of military rules. The labyrinth has always been about Sarah's journey as a human. There are monsters and friendly worms to meet along

the way, but even when you reach the labyrinth's heart, there's always another layer, another turn, another *experience.*

## GREENNESS AND VISIBILITY

In *Labyrinth*, green remains an eerie background color, part of the rust-and-gold palette of the richly designed sets. But it does make a central appearance in the Bog of Eternal Stench, one of the film's extended jokes that ends up marrying horror with childish glee. Jareth continually threatens Hoggle with the bog, and when Sarah asks what the big deal is — *Does it just stink?* — he emphatically replies: "That's enough . . . and the worst thing is, if you set even one foot in the Bog of Eternal Stench, it'll never come out. You'll smell bad *for the rest of your life.*" Both Froud and Brian Henson have mused that this whole idea was aimed at child audiences. It was the kind of humor that Sarah, as a teenager, would have found repulsive, while a younger version of her might have laughed at it. But Jim Henson took an almost unreasonable amount of entertainment from the bog. He had fart noises designed on a synthesizer, and he laughed uncontrollably when Sir Didymus rides his sheepdog-steed Ambrosius across the rocks, each of them farting in turn. According to Brian Henson, this was his father's favorite part of the movie. An artist spending resources to craft the perfect fart joke is, perhaps, the most accurate definition of Henson as a director and storyteller. In the midst of a dramatic scene, he still wanted to play.

I remember rewatching *Labyrinth* as a grad student — we'd all been drinking at a party and wanted to revisit a childhood classic. None of us were certain if the film would hold up, and in some ways it didn't, because we weren't the same people who'd fallen in love with it as kids. But the fart noises made us laugh. We shook and tried not to spill our wine because grad school was like that: horrifying, tragicomic, ridiculous. A failed queer thesis. A drinking problem. A miniature sheepdog dancing across a fart joke. That's what we were. Characters lost in an academic labyrinth, hoping to see some crack of light that led to an outside.

The bog was made of a Jell-O-like substance that resembled raw toothpaste. It was unruly. The viscous liquid was only several inches deep in most places, but in *Labyrinth: A Visual History*, Brian Henson notes a dark corner of the set that became like the deep end of a pool. A camera operator fell in once, and tried to pull himself up by a chain, but it was slick with bog goo. He was so worried about ruining the $100,000 camera that he allowed himself to sink while holding the piece of equipment aloft until someone could grab it. "He was in over his head," Henson observed.[34]

I can think of few metaphors that more accurately capture the experience of grad school. I was teaching classes at age 21. I could still barely get out of bed in the morning, and the world was a crush of bright light and painful sound. I didn't know how to talk to other people, and I was eating granola

34 *Labyrinth* Blu-ray featurette.

bars for supper, but I also had to explain the symbolism of *Oedipus Rex* to a room full of bored undergraduate students. Our collective anxiety spilled over, like that bog. What were we doing with all of these books and ideas? Would any of us get full-time jobs? We needed Ludo to call the rocks from the depths, to form a path of escape. But the bog was still there, always. A cauldron of uncertainty, staining our lives green. Just like Gawain, who retains the green knight's scar on the delicate flesh of his neck.

Last summer, I decided to scathe myself on purpose with a tattoo. It's an image from a twelfth-century medieval bestiary: a winged siren. I modified the image, so that the siren has a smooth chest, making her trans-femme. An inscription wraps around her bird talons: *Se Elianorum nominans*. This refers to a fifteenth-century trans sex worker named Eleanor Rykener, whose life was partially recorded in a Latin deposition after she was arrested. She corrected the scribe on her name, and so he added the note: *She called herself Eleanor*. A woman marked and scathed by the transphobia of her era, but still, living a life. The scales of my siren are a rich blue-green. My tattoo artist, also trans, said: *This shading might hurt, but it will look great . . .* The blood that swelled under the aftercare bandage was my own personal bog.

*

Henson's clearest association with the color green comes from his famous song "It's Not Easy Bein' Green," which Kermit

sings while wandering through the forest. He thinks about how nice it would be if he were another color. He blends in rather than standing out. If he were to flee the embrace of the leaves, the color is precisely what would make him different. What does it mean to be green in a city, or a crowded room? Is green all there is? Should he be something else? *Why wonder*, he murmurs. It's perfect Hensonian delivery: not quite a question, and no answer in sight. Of course we have to wonder. His body of work is a starfall of wondering, a gorgeous exploration of life's questions through puppetry, fairy tale, and radical dreaming. Kermit ends the song by asserting that green is beautiful. That *he* is beautiful. But there's a note of uncertainty, as there always is in Henson's work. He *thinks* green is what he might want to be. Can we ever know for sure?

However, Henson was certain about one thing: that *Labyrinth* would be an acclaimed success in North America, even though most critics would eventually fail to see the imaginative power and wild sense of play that he'd poured into the film. They saw it as a surface that reflected nothing. After all that touring, all those press interviews, how could he have been so wrong about the film's reception?

I'd argue that this mirrors my own experience of being autistic. Not just feeling green, but so often being surprised by the world and its reactions. Growing up, what I wanted more than anything was Kermit's green camouflage, like a benevolent Romulan cloaking device. Let me vanish into the leaves and be invisible to predators! But the green stuck to me no matter where I was. People could spot the difference on me a mile

away, and they made it clear that I should change my coloration, or risk being a social exile.

Now I try to see green for all of its delightful paradoxes. Sometimes I fuck up socially, and people notice. Sometimes I blend in. Some days I'm a bog witch, struggling to complete even a single human task.

Everyone in *Labyrinth* runs from the bog, yet it's also a source of comedy, a moment of farty joy. What if we dove right in, like the brave camera operator? Let the bog scathe and soak us? We could say that Henson was touched by the green of the bog. Sometimes he stood out when he wanted to blend in; and sometimes he was invisible when he wanted to shine.

The blessing of being marked by bog-green is an unexpected lesson that I've taken from the film, while working on this book. Dip a toe into the bog. It's not so bad. You'll smell different, but maybe you'll become what you've always wanted.

*

*Labyrinth* shows us that it's okay to be green and dripping. There are untold ichors and substances sloshing around in our bodies, and they're all necessary. Being green makes you visible in ways that are sometimes uncomfortable. But why would you be anything but who you are? In the CBC show *Sort Of*, when Bilal Baig's character is told that being trans is a dangerous life, they respond: "I don't know. Life is always dangerous. I feel like it's an honest life."

Go ahead, the film says, be green. Let your insides show. Imagine a drop of green blood, hovering like a capillary miracle on your finger. If we're going to survive at all, let us be a monstrous family. You've never been more sure of anything.

# 5

## *Labyrinth* and the Contradictions of Eighties Cinema

The eighties produced a boom of fantasy-action films that incorporated early CGI, evolving prosthetics tech, and puppetry techniques pioneered by Henson Studios. It's often described as a golden age of fantastic cinema: *Legend*, *Labyrinth*, *The Neverending Story*, *The Last Starfighter*, *The Explorers*, *Flight of the Navigator*, *Beetlejuice*. Films that transformed young viewers on a cellular level, turning them toward dragons, sandworms, and stars. These stories were concerned with the power of imagination, and though some of them included lessons (*Legend* feels a bit like a morality play with ecological highlights), many of them celebrated the breakdown of the "real" world. Sarah brings the goblins home with her. Bastian flies Falkor through the streets of downtown Vancouver. Lydia

dances with ghosts in the triumphant end to *Beetlejuice*. There was the sense that you could survive this world, if only you preserved a connection to the weird and the wondrous. A perfect byline for the mercantile capitalism of the eighties: *The world sucks, but there are dragons!*

In reality, the eighties were close to unbearable for anyone who wasn't a movie star or a white venture capitalist. Ronald Reagan was shaping America into a white Christian theocracy, while Brian Mulroney's conservative government was leading Canada toward a recession. Historian Doug Rossinow notes that Reaganism was embodied by "unfettered capitalism," as well as corporate fraud and a massive expansion of the prison complex. In 1983, Reagan proudly announced that "[America] is a country where someone can always get rich."[35] This was a time when people unironically used the term "progressive conservative" to describe someone who might not kick you out of the house for being gay, but would definitely withhold funding from AIDS research. In her 1992 essay "The Denial of AIDS," Sarah Schulman writes: "The America that is against us is composed of and maintained by our families."[36] People were routinely rejected after coming out. Queer communities were fighting against a mixture of public disinformation, religious oppression on both the family and state level, and the unchecked greed of pharmaceutical companies. It was a perfect storm of the neoliberal elements that defined the era:

35 Rossinow, *The Reagan Era*, 6.

36 Schulman, *My American History*, 236.

capitalist expansion and deregulation, televangelism and the rise of the megachurch, and the consolidation of corporate wealth masquerading as meritocracy (a term still invoked by the 2025 Trump regime).

By 1986, when *Labyrinth* hit theaters, 25,000 people had already died of AIDS in the United States,[37] including Rock Hudson. In Canada, around 700 people were dying per year,[38] and the Canadian AIDS Society had only just been established. Around this time, I remember watching a show with my dad called *Spitting Image*, which satirized politics by using puppets. It was so popular that the puppets made an appearance in a Genesis video, where they wandered through a "land of confusion." In the episode I specifically remember watching, Ronald Reagan was in bed with Nancy, tweezing the hair from his ears. They both talked in squeaky, ridiculous voices, and my dad laughed hugely. It was a moment of comedic body horror during a time when our bodies had actually become horror films.

Even that young, I knew that I was queer and that AIDS was killing the generation of people who might have taught me something about myself. But we laughed, because it was easier to mock the confusion than to actually feel its profound depth. I didn't know, at the time, that artists-turned-activists like David Wojnarowicz had already crafted a searing body of

---

37 This statistic is based on the *amfAR* website, organized by the AIDS/HIV-advocacy group that tracks U.S. policy decisions.

38 This statistic comes from the Government of Canada document "AIDS: Medical and Scientific Aspects," published by Sonya Norris et al. in 2001.

work designed to make AIDS mortality visible, not just a blip on TV, but flesh and bone. In his 1989 essay "Post Cards from America," he writes about his anger and the need for public mourning:

> I imagine what it would be like if friends had a demonstration each time a lover or friend or stranger died of AIDS. I imagine what it would be like if, each time a lover, friend or stranger died of this disease, their friends, lovers or neighbors would take their dead body and drive with it in a car a hundred miles to washington dc and blast through the gates of the white house and come to a screeching halt before the entrance and then dump their lifeless forms on the front steps.[39]

We watched news reports about ACT UP and Queer Nation, but Chilliwack, my hometown, felt like a fairy-tale village, as shielded from conflict as Sarah's suburb in *Labyrinth*. I wouldn't come out to my dad until the late nineties, during my first year of college. The group of protease-inhibitor drugs known as the cocktail was being refined, and it was now possible to live a relatively healthy life as an HIV+ person. I was terrified of sex — not just from the constant specter of AIDS, but because my body was full of intensities. The world was a sensory nightmare, I could barely look another person in the

39 Wojnarowicz, *Witnesses: Against Our Vanishing*, 11.

eye (it felt so intimate), and kissing a boy had not changed my life in the way I'd hoped it would.

Those spectacular eighties films taught me that you needed fantasy to survive. That goblins and shadows and luck dragons were hiding below every surface, just waiting for me to find them. Because what I wanted — what so many queer kids wanted, above all else — was a magic that would guarantee our survival. We didn't need a thousand wishes from a childlike empress. We just wanted to get through another day without feeling like we'd been born on the wrong planet.

In the much darker second half of the novel *The Neverending Story*, Bastian has to re-create Fantastica. Through a series of questionable wishes, he takes on the role of the childlike empress: the immortal girl in the ivory tower. She's the prime mover of Fantastica — something older and wiser than anyone else. Bastian doesn't even fully understand how much he wants her power until he has it. Michael Ende's book, especially the German original, is just as much about tyranny and soulless corporate brainwashing as it is about luck dragons and depressed horses. Ende's fantasy couldn't exist without the sobering realities of capitalism. It's as if we need fantasy in order to persevere. Because we do.

I could be a problematic empress. A disaster goblin. Meg Mucklebones from *Legend*, who saw Tom Cruise as a tasty morsel. A clear-eyed girl finding her way to the heart of a labyrinth, in search of a new queer family.

Aside from David Bowie, I had two other queer awakenings as an eighties kid: one predictable, the other a bit more obscure. The first was Tim Curry as horny Darkness in the film *Legend*. If you haven't seen it, *Legend* is a 1985 film by Ridley Scott that was plagued by disaster. The painfully constructed medieval forest set burned down. Actor Robert Picardo nearly drowned while playing the aquatic monster Meg Mucklebones. The film had two different scores, and multiple cuts, none of which satisfied Scott. The writers were flying high on cocaine and kept pitching increasingly bizarre and impossible ideas, including a version where Tom Cruise was entirely painted green. It's a film about purity that ends with a Bryan Ferry music video. It's a film about unicorns, goblins, and fairies, with a haunting score by Tangerine Dream (or Jerry Goldsmith, depending on which version you watch). *Legend* forms part of what I've come to think of as the holy trinity of eighties fantasy films, with *Labyrinth* and *Neverending Story* as its partners in sacred crime. I was seduced by the unicorns with their wobbly horns, the playfully sadistic goblins, and a twinky Tom Cruise leaping around the forest in gold chainmail and a loincloth.

Then I saw Darkness.

There's a popular saying about Tim Curry and his role in *Muppet Treasure Island* (please stay with me). He's successful because he *is* a muppet. Curry has always had the ability to vanish into characters, and he plays Darkness — a jacked version of Lucifer — with a kind of menacing charm. Imagine if

Dr. Frank-N-Furter had actually achieved a dark apotheosis and become the devil. Even under literal pounds of prosthetic makeup, with horns and hooves and contact lenses that nearly blinded him, Curry was an iconic prince of evil. Sitting on his throne, bored and horny and hating joy like a deeply confusing Grinch in hell, you could tell that he was absolutely up for anything. As he fills cups with black wine, his claws drum the table in an-tici-pation. I wanted Darkness to invite me to dinner. His clawed hands could gently apply black lipstick, which would taste like emptiness. Fuck those unicorns. Let's dance and burn to sinister keyboard music.

Perhaps the most unsettling moment in *Legend* features a mysterious dance. Darkness asks his father (whoever that is) for advice on how to seduce Lily, played by a willowy but defiant Mia Sara. *Charm her*, a creepy voice tells him. So far, dinner dates and threats haven't worked. So Darkness tries something else. He summons a shadow-dancer, dressed all in black, with their face completely covered. Their gender is liquid. They dance with Lily to a dark techno waltz, and while she's scared at first, she eventually takes the lead. They spin and flash with light, and suddenly, Lily becomes the dancer. Now her hair is the color of a raven's feather, lips black as night. She is unquestionably powerful. And possibly evil.

I watched this scene over and over. Who was the dancer? Was it Darkness himself, in another form? One of his goblins, under some kind of spell? Or was Lily dancing with a queer version of herself, like John Donne's poem about Sappho in the mirror? *Myself I embrace, and mine own hands I kiss.* In a

film with Tim Curry strutting and raging and cackling, this still manages to be the gayest scene. And it filled me with a different kind of desire. I wanted to be that dark dancer, swaying between genders. I wanted to be Mia Sara but also the shadow spinning her. I wasn't Darkness, or Lily, or Jack. I was someone in between. A backup dancer in hell, with the power to glide however they desired.

## *BEETLEJUICE* AND RADICAL GAY DECORATORS

The second awakening was a bit more subtle, but no less important. When *Beetlejuice* premiered in 1987, my parents drove me to see it at the Capitol 6 Theatre on Granville Street, in the heart of the Vancouver's downtown core. Granville[40] is often described as being stubbornly "old Vancouver," a space that resists the slick style of gentrification that has flattened out many of the city's most complex neighborhoods. The neon lights of the Vogue and Orpheum theaters are a reminder of Granville's role as the historic entertainment district, and those spaces once thrived as vaudeville theaters on Hastings Street, as well. In the late eighties, you could still see cheap movies on Granville, and the Capitol 6 Theatre — *six* whole screens! — was a wild adventure compared with my sleepy life in Chilliwack. When you rode the escalator to the

40 Granville was also the original name for Vancouver, before it mostly burned down in the late nineteenth century. The area now called Gastown — which was mostly designed in the seventies — still retains some original elements from the days when Vancouver was organized around lumber mills and saloons.

top floor, you could see the city below, a web of stories and burning neon.

*Beetlejuice* was one of the first movies I can remember that had a distinct marketing push. The jangling soundtrack, the bloody-but-fun special effects, the eventual cartoon and line of toys: it was an event. I sat next to my mother and stepfather, who, at the time, were both still capable of enjoying each other's company. It was early in their relationship, a period marked by rock concerts, movies, and nights watching *ALF*. We laughed as a furry extraterrestrial did his best to catch and eat the family cat. We all seemed to prosper beneath the warm glow of various screens, big and small. Everything was popcorn and possibility.

*Beetlejuice* focuses on the Deetz family and their attempts to renovate a haunted house. Along the way, Lydia Deetz — played iconically as a Goth waif by Winona Ryder — bonds with the recently deceased couple who used to live in their new house. Catherine O'Hara, the family's artistic matriarch, spends most of the time screaming about how nobody is honoring her moody aesthetic. In many ways, the film is about eighties gentrification, as much as it's also a satire about the afterlife. The title character embodies everything we find unpleasant about dying: he eats bugs while actively decaying, and he's distressingly horny for a corpse.

What the film is most definitely *not* about is the family's interior decorator — a minor character named Otho, played by Glenn Shadix. He only has a few noteworthy scenes, and he's mostly a figure of comic relief. To me, though, he was the

unexpected heart of the film. I couldn't take my eyes off this person, who was big, bold, cutting, funny, and . . . something else. The word I'd use now is *queer*, but at the time, I simply understood him to be different. One of the charms of *Beetlejuice* is that nobody has to fall in love. The film ends with a horrific wedding interrupted by a sandworm, and Lydia — unlike most teen girls in popular films of the era — focuses on getting good grades rather than dating boys. Tim Burton, the film's director, loves dysfunctional families, and the Deetz family is a wonderful mess. What captured my attention, though, was the question of Otho and how he related to Deetzes. Who was he, to them, exactly?

He begins by climbing dramatically through a window, then lecturing Catherine O'Hara's character, Delia, about how much his renovation is going to cost. From the first moment on-screen, Shadix imbues Otho with a sense of power and aggressive confidence. The buttons of his cardigan are blood red. In a later scene, he wears a silk robe on their balcony, while drinking a cocktail, and proclaims: "I know just as much about the supernatural as I do about interior design." Every scene between Shadix and O'Hara is comic gold, and it's a delight to watch their comedic styles dancing with each other. Delia is the film's most dramatic character, but Otho still manages to upstage her with one-liners and deft physical comedy. Before the famous dinner scene — when Beetlejuice possesses the guests and forces them to sing a Harry Belafonte song — Otho jokes darkly about suicide and dominates the conversation in a breezy, powerful way. One of Delia's guests

makes a comment about Otho's type of person (*your kind*), and he immediately responds with a joke about the wicked witch from *The Wizard of Oz*. When faced with a particular kind of upper-class homophobia, he simply reverses the interaction, so that everyone is laughing with him. *Beetlejuice* was filmed at the height of the AIDS crisis, and while Burton doesn't comment on this directly, he does make the choice to cast an openly gay actor in a visibly gay role.

In some ways, Otho is an expansion of Bronson Pinchot's scene-stealing gay clerk in *Beverly Hills Cop*, whose performance is so wry and brilliant that Eddie Murphy struggles to keep up with him. Murphy was well known for his homophobic rant in the popular comedy special *Delirious* (something he's since apologized for), and it's particularly satisfying to see this micro-character snatch the scene out from under him. In *Beetlejuice*, Otho has multiple scenes to steal, and while he may be played for laughs, the humor is gentler than we'd expect for an eighties comedy. There's a moment where Michael Keaton's sadistic ghoul could do anything he wants to Otho, but he chooses to dress him in a hideous baby-blue suit. Otho screams in horror, and the audience laughs, because of course this homosexual's greatest fear is wearing polyester. Burton is doing what the gender theorist Judith Butler (I'll bet you didn't expect me to connect them to *Beetlejuice*!) calls "working the weakness within the norm."[41] He's mining a vein of eighties homophobic humor around the figure of the gay

41 This phrase comes from their 2004 book, *Undoing Gender*.

interior decorator but also challenging us to see Otho as a beloved human character.

When his spell to capture spirits haunting their house goes wrong, and we're forced to watch Geena Davis's character crumbling to dust before our eyes, Otho feels visible remorse. "I'm sorry," he whispers to the ghost, which is a lot more than Delia ever says. He runs away in the end, but he also survives. Deep in our hearts, we know that he's still sharing cocktails with Delia and thinking about everything mauve paint can do. He's treated with more dignity and care than most gay roles of the time, and Shadix plays him as a defiantly visible gay man who literally makes a joke about closets. I knew I was supposed to care about the big moments in the film, but for nine-year-old me, Otho *was* the big moment. A character unlike any I'd seen before on a massive screen. He haunted me in the best possible way, and sometimes I imagine Glenn Shadix lip-synching to "Magic Dance" from *Labyrinth*. A goblin king and a ghoul queen, both gleefully derailing plots, stealing scenes, and radicalizing queer small-town kids with their magic.

## *LABYRINTH* AND QUEER FAIRY TALES

Stepmothers are often evil in fairy tales, because a woman who marries a widower is suspect. The original mother — often dead — is a saint. The stepmother is the devil who casts her spell over the unsuspecting family. Think of Cinderella's stepmother, who locks her in a world of endless labor. In *Ever*

*After*, the nineties adaptation of Perrault's conte, Anjelica Huston plays the evil stepmother with deliciously acid charm. She shames one of her daughters for being fat (a label that would follow Melanie Lynskey's career as she dealt with the full force of late-nineties fatphobia) and mocks the other for being dim of wit. But her most ruthless attacks are reserved for Drew Barrymore's plucky heroine, Danielle, who memorably fends off an old predator by holding a knife to his privates.

There's only one scene where Anjelica Huston's character, Rodmilla, drops her cold mask and has a human interaction with Danielle. She touches Danielle's cheek, unexpectedly, and says how much she looks like her father. We see, in this moment, that Rodmilla may be an evil, capitalist widow, but she still misses her husband. And is it wrong of her to secure a fortune for her daughters? She cruelly mistreats Danielle, but there's something fierce in her evil mothering. Unlike the original story, which forces her to dance to death in a pair of metal shoes, the film merely relegates her (and her daughter Marguerite) to working in the castle laundry. Melanie Lynskey's character, Jacqueline, is spared because she has always been kind to Danielle. She meets a royal page at a masquerade, and they bond over their shared love of buffets. Is it fatphobic? Probably. But there's something gentle about the way that they flirt in their final scene together. Maybe they're still part of a nineties joke, but they're in control of the joke. They find romantic possibility as two characters who aren't deemed to be "traditionally" attractive by the film, in spite of the fact that they're both cute as hell, and arguably more interesting than the central characters.

The film includes Leonardo da Vinci as a misfit inventor, along with Danielle's friend, Gustave, who eventually becomes his apprentice. Da Vinci was famously queer and had a long-term relationship with his apprentice Salai (feel free to check out his erotic portrait of Salai — just not while you're at work). Gustave has zero chemistry with Danielle — he's a dreamer, helping out da Vinci with his experiments, while awkwardly loping through the film's background. *Ever After* came out in 1998, a year after the brief Renaissance in marketable gay films that brought us *In and Out* and the (far superior) *My Best Friend's Wedding*. I knew that *Ever After* probably wouldn't acknowledge da Vinci's queerness, but I fully expected Gustave to have a coming-out moment. He doesn't.

But I'd argue that the film allows him to be queer-coded, through his association with da Vinci, as well as his close friendship with Danielle. If we imagine *Ever After* to be an adaptation of da Vinci as a historical figure, than Gustave *is* Salai. Both of them are goblincore in the film, with their ratty tunics, unkempt hair, and focus on scientific wonder rather than romance. For me, having come out only a couple of years earlier, the film offered both a revisionist fairy tale and an alternative to heterosexual romance: become da Vinci's queer apprentice instead. Build a flying machine that will carry you to a masquerade, where you can be exactly who you are behind the mask that you choose for yourself.

*

There's a moment at the beginning of *Labyrinth* where Sarah confronts her stepmother. A teen girl stands in the doorway of her suburban home, dripping wet. She could be Elizabeth Bennet in *Pride and Prejudice*, muddy and soaked through after her long walk to Bingley's manor.

In *American Cinema of the 1980s*, Leger Grindon notes that 1986 produced several films that were focused on the decaying foundations of suburban America, including David Lynch's brilliant *Blue Velvet*. While a more popular film like *Ferris Bueller's Day Off* celebrates what Grindon calls "teen omnipotence," *Labyrinth* seems more interested in Sarah's fragility as a suburban teen girl in the Reagan Eighties. Her stepmother is a magazine photo of classic eighties fashion: pearls, perfectly waved hair, a pink blouse with billowing half-moon sleeves, and a power belt. Her lipstick is the same color as the Fireys. Sarah, by contrast, wears a damp Victorian gown with limp tassels. As they face each other beneath an expensive chandelier, her stepmother says in a sour tone: "Oh, *Sarah*." It might as well be a refrain of familial disappointment. Sarah doesn't fit within their expensive house, their capitalist life. She has too many weird outfits, too many toys and picture books and games. She's dripping on the plush carpet. She is an arbiter of decay.

This scene always makes me think of another late-eighties classic, *Uncle Buck*, where Tia faces down her mother. But Tia is every inch an eighties teen, with her bangs and severe scarves. She always thinks she's in control, until her boyfriend, the aptly named Bug, tries to assault her and her terminally uncool uncle rescues her. At the end of the movie, she reconciles with her

mother — fiercely and unexpectedly hugging her. "Everything's going to be different," her mother says. And we believe it, because Buck, like some kind of goblin prince, has cast a spell of charm and goodwill over their lives. Everyone can finally relax because suburbia will remain intact.

Was *Labyrinth* an aberration within a landscape of conservative eighties cinema, or was it firmly a story of its time? Films like *Rambo* and *Rocky*, which were far more popular, belonged to a tradition known as the New Cold War Cinema: an expression of America's imperialist values that were translated onto movie screens. But there were still many titles that challenged the neo-conservative order. Cinema scholar Stephen Prince notes that "although the Reagan presidency excelled at ideological production, Hollywood film was neither mono-dimensional nor coterminous with the politics of those years."[42] Henson's films, in particular, criticized notions of dictatorship (the Skeksis in *The Dark Crystal*) and unreasonable consumption (think of Sarah's room in *Labyrinth*, packed with toys).

While films like *Legend* focused on defeating sexy evil and restoring a purity symbolized by unicorns, the ending of *Labyrinth* is far more nuanced. There's no climactic battle between Sarah and the Goblin King. They talk. They match wits. They confront each other psychologically, as the world falls down around them. The film reminds child viewers that their most powerful weapon is their minds and the labyrinth is meant to be experienced, not merely solved. Life isn't a piece

42 Prince, "Genres and Production Cycles," 342.

of cake — it's dark and full of sinister passageways — but that doesn't mean the joy and pain aren't worth it. Perhaps eighties audiences would have preferred Sarah to climb into an F-16 fighter jet, and pummel the Goblin King with missiles. Or be saved at the last minute by a benevolent John Candy and safely installed, once again, in her suburban bedroom. Instead, she reaches the castle beyond the Goblin City, and she does it alone.

Nobody puts a gun in her hand. She doesn't climb into an exoskeleton. But she doesn't run either. She faces complexity head on, and, in Brian Froud's words, "remembers what she's always known." She doesn't need the power of Grayskull, or any other fantasy element, or, even, the trappings of capitalism, because the power of radical choice is within her.

# 6

## Jim Henson's Masquerade

I don't want to say that Henson was autistic. But I will say that our brains would have gotten along like . . . well . . . brains on fire.

Lately, I've been talking a lot with my students about the term *neuroqueer*, which was popularized by autistic scholars Nick Walker and M. Remi Yergeau. Walker describes the concept as "approaching, embodying, and/or experiencing one's neurodivergence as a form of queerness."[43] Your brain can be queer, just as your bodies, desires, and cultural affiliations can be queer. This has always made sense to me, since most of my queer and trans friends are also neurodivergent (though

43 This comes from their online essay "Neuroqueer: An Introduction" and can be explored further as a concept in their 2021 book *Neuroqueer Heresies*.

there's no "correct" brain to diverge *from*, so even that term needs work). Regardless of how Henson understood himself, I *get* his brain, and a lot of autistic and ADHD folks also get him in intimate ways.

Henson grew up in a Christian Scientist household, and these beliefs would one day impact his health (his instinct was never to go to the hospital). But they also made him open to mysticism and transcendental possibilities, and you can see that in his work. Are the Muppets queer and anti-capitalist? Heck yes. When Kermit sings "Rainbow Connection," we imagine a kinder world, not defined by consumption, open to many different desires and experiences. What we don't realize is that Henson endangered his own life to deliver that scene. He pretzeled himself into a diving bell, in an underwater tank, so that Kermit would appear to play the guitar on his lily pad. That was Henson in a nutshell: doing the most difficult and elaborate work possible in order to create an image of gorgeous simplicity, building the world's biggest mechanized puppet who emerged from the door of the Goblin King's castle in *Labyrinth* purely for a five-minute scene of chaos and delight.

Henson's brother died young, and he was obsessed with the idea of the body as a ticking time bomb — we could all wink out at any moment. The clock in *Labyrinth*, measuring Sarah's progress, was an old theme in his work. One of his first hybrid videos focused on a clock counting down and the fear of not being able to accomplish everything. When Jareth languidly points to the clock, and shaves off a few precious hours, Sarah yells: *That's not* fair*!* He looks at her pitilessly and says: *You're*

*right. And maybe that's the point.* Henson understood mortality in an uncomfortable way, and his more mature works tried to translate that for audiences, often with mixed results.

In the documentary *Idea Man*, actress Rita Moreno talks about Henson's social awkwardness — particularly his discomfort with interviews. "I don't know if it was shyness. Jim was a reticent person when it came to communicating with people." His mind was often on other things, like characters. One of his early collaborators, IBM executive David Lazer, recalls walking with Henson one evening after an important meeting. He seemed distracted, and Lazer assumed he was thinking about budgets or proposals, all the business details they had talked about that day. But Henson was actually just captivated by the motion of the moonlight on water as they passed.[44]

Co-workers described his incredible willpower, and he was famously stubborn, but he also had the patience and warmth to work with very young children. Henson was a paradox, and there was something comforting about his resolute strangeness. I can empathize with his desire to stand out while also needing to remain invisible to predators, a hunger for fame and attention coupled with a squeamishness about appearing on camera. I'd argue that a lot of neurodiverse folks experience this exact paradox: wanting to be seen and also fearing it at the same time.

Henson once said: "Puppets are a lot like masks. Children — and adults — can perform without inhibitions. And without

44 Jones, *Jim Henson*, 315.

being seen."[45] He was an artist, entrepreneur, and storyteller who was always uncomfortable on-camera without a puppet as a mediator. The type of performer who'd nearly suffocate by climbing into a diving bell to animate Kermit's guitar for the "Rainbow Connection" song, but would also hide his face and slouch into chairs whenever he was interviewed. He lived apart from his wife and collaborator, Jane, for years, but would not agree to an official divorce — only a separation for the benefit of their public image. He refused to pay his own children overtime for working long hours in his studio, but also instilled within them a sense of dignity, empathy, and seriousness for the art that they were creating.

Like her creator, Sarah in *Labyrinth* prefers masks and costumes to direct conflict. In spite of Jennifer Connelly's marketable, middle-class white beauty, her character has an aesthetic that's almost frumpy. Worn jeans, a Victorian blouse, minimal makeup (she irritably tosses away a tube of lipstick). This could be a chaste view of girlhood on Henson's part, but it also reads as a nerdy white everygirl who just wants to read fantasy novels and LARP in the park. When Jareth remakes Sarah into a kind of dreamy Gothic princess, it feels like someone else's fantasy. Sarah is far more comfortable returning to her original look, which seems calculated to be ordinary so that the audience will focus on her mind, rather than her outfit. Though she's trying to solve the labyrinth, it seems clear that a part of her wants to stay lost within it. The outside world is full of expectations

45 Ibid., 377.

and the traumatic slide toward adulthood. In the labyrinth, she dwells in a kind of twilight childhood. Masked and free.

## QUEER MINDS AND EIGHTEENTH-CENTURY MASQUERADES

During the final promotional wave for *Labyrinth*, Jim Henson held a masquerade ball at his home in London. In fact, he often hosted masquerades and has said in interviews that he felt more comfortable behind a mask — it was a lot like puppeteering.[46] He'd glide around his London home in a goblin mask, checking on guests, making jokes, doing everything but actually appearing as himself. Henson's life was, really, a masquerade ball: he crafted friendly puppets but was privately filled with grief over the early death of his older brother.

Henson was deeply, often wonderfully complicated, and I can think of no better metaphor than a masquerade to represent that complexity. A space where you could be yourself by paradoxically *not* being yourself. A parquet floor where you could dance with monsters and princesses and beautiful, unsettling truths encased in crystal. There's joy at the core of it, but also a kind of serious play that often defines how we face the world — with many different faces.

I teach courses in eighteenth-century literature, and the masquerade was a central idea within that era. Literary scholar

46 Ibid.

Terry Castle describes it as perhaps the strongest organizing principle within such a stratified society — the idea of disrupting the rigid public/private divide through a kind of twilight performance. "The pleasures and dangers of the masquerade were of a particularly revelatory kind."[47]

As any queer person who has experienced Halloween can tell you, putting on a costume often allows you to discover a truth about yourself. We still have costume parties, and for some it's just a bit of fun, but for others it's life-defining. In the eighteenth century, a masquerade ball was one of the only places where queer and trans people had the freedom to appear as themselves. Images from the period display a startling variety of costumes, from monsters and milkmaids to chess pieces and literal hedges. In John Cleland's famously banned *Memoirs of a Woman of Pleasure*, a man encounters Emily, a cross-dressed sex worker, at a masquerade. He's then disappointed to discover that she's a cis woman ("By heavens, a woman!"), and Emily is also annoyed, but the whole business is treated with a kind of affection. *These things happen at masquerades.*

Cleland's book was particularly censured for its depiction of sex between men, which was still an offense punishable by hanging in 1748, when the book was published. In fact, the book emerged after a series of violent raids on queer spaces — molly houses — which were the ancestor to the modern gay bar. Like the famous Stonewall Inn, these private bars survived through a mixture of secrecy, collaboration, and payoffs to the

47 Castle, *Masquerade and Civilization*, 4.

authorities of the day. The more queer and trans people resisted attempts to destroy their community, the more visible — and simultaneously vulnerable — they became.

On a trip to London early in my job as an instructor, I visited a few sites that we're reasonably certain used to be molly houses. I worked with information from the scholarship of Alan Bray and Rictor Norton, who have both devoted considerable study to these spaces and how they changed over time. Bray died young, but Rictor Norton still maintains a vital open-access website full of primary sources on London's queer history. I visited a pub called the Red Dragon, close to the area once known as Saffron Hill, which Bray described as a collection of "unsanitary warrens" full of alleys and dive bars. I took a photo of the Red Dragon, which could only be entered through a dark tunnel. Water dripped down cracks in the stone, and I tried to imagine an eighteenth-century molly, delicately lifting the train of their skirt so it wouldn't drag across the wet stones (one of the possible origins of the word *drag*, which circulated as early as the seventeenth century).

Writer Julia Ftacek is careful to note that when scholars insist on the mollies being cis gay men, this "comes at the foreclosure of any possibility that anything resembling transgender identity could also be found among individuals in the molly subculture."[48] Historians often argue that something like "queer consciousness," or a sense of one's own sexuality as *identity*, didn't emerge until the nineteenth century — perhaps

48 Ftacek, "Jonathan Swift and the Transgender Classroom," 304.

with the brutally public trial of Oscar Wilde. But from what we can tell, both the men and trans women who called themselves *mollies* were connecting their desires and relationships with a visible community. When William Brown was arrested for sodomy in 1726, he said: "There is no crime in making what use I please of my own body." The mollies who frequented these private spaces would often put on drag performances and dress up in high fashion, creating their own kind of masquerade: not a costume party, but a crystalline image of who they were. When a trans woman named Princess Seraphina was arrested for stealing back her clothes from a lover, the community spoke up for her, and she was released. London, with its brilliance and shadows, felt like a masquerade at times, but the bonds of queer community were vital and real.

Henson was an introvert but he also hosted masquerades that filled the massive ballroom at the Waldorf-Astoria hotel. This makes sense to me as an instructor, since many instructors are introverts who are expected to "perform" for set periods of time. Like a masquerade ball, a classroom is a space for transformation, which can include unexpected moments. But the space is still under the instructor's control, just as Henson's masked balls were something that *he* organized. A space for conditional chaos, where the social order might be upset, but only for a short time. Gliding among his guests while wearing a mask was very different from sitting down to answer specific questions about his work and life. Both masks and puppets offered Henson a way of appearing in public while still wearing a creative disguise.

The masquerade ball is one of *Labyrinth*'s most complex set pieces, along with the battle at the Goblin City. But while the battle was supposed to be comic, the masquerade is ethereal and unsettling, like a dream you can barely understand. Elliot Scott, the set designer, wanted to create an "eighteenth-century Venetian ball," where everyone was "vaguely depraved," which feels slightly odd in a film for children. He understood puppetry as the complex art form that it was, and the ball scene illustrates that fairy-tale tension between dreamy childhood and a darker world beyond. Brian Froud, who worked with Henson to develop *Labyrinth* from the ground up, notes that the humans in the ball scene are "gentry playing at being goblins,"[49] just as eighteenth-century masquerade-goers were often powerful socialites reaching for a different kind of power: anonymity and fluidity. After an hour of narrative time where Sarah is the only human on camera, the ball scene presents us with nothing but humans — but are they really? Or are they Jareth's goblins in disguise? Part of the magic of *Labyrinth* is that it queers the ideas of *human* and *monster*, such as the moment when Sarah says to Ludo: "You seem like such a nice beast." In this dream world, there's little distinction between human and goblin, since she's learning to unmask the artificial calculus that decides what it means to be a person — something Henson does in all of his work.

49 *Labyrinth* Blu-ray featurette.

In the film's featurette, Henson describes the ballroom scene as "Sarah's fantasy," but this raises a number of questions about what she really wants. She's a 14-year-old girl who spends most of her time acting out scenes from this world, but never this scene, in particular. When we see her in the park, she's performing the final scene of defiance — the moment when she realizes that the Goblin King has no power over her — not this creepy masquerade, full of glitter and dread.

The film often seems to steer her toward a problematic romance with the presumably immortal Goblin King, made irresistible by David Bowie's enormously charming performance (and his iconic status as a bisexual demigod). But in spite of the film's subtext, Sarah never demonstrates a clear romantic interest in Jareth. She's scared of him, annoyed with him, defiant toward his petulant and despotic rule — but I'd argue that Jennifer Connelly doesn't play their connection as romantic in any conscious way. Like her parents, Jareth is one more force of perverse authority keeping her from spending her time as she likes. That's his central power, in fact: he's always cheating time. Jareth even scolds her at the end of the film, saying that he's "re-altered time" for her, the sort of thing a stalker-y male sonneteer would say to a baffled woman: *Look at all the things I've done for you*. Sarah's only real wish was for her baby brother to disappear, and she immediately regretted it. So it's unclear how this weird ball-in-a-ball is her adolescent fantasy. If anything, it's Jareth's fantasy, which she literally shatters when she throws a chair through the glass surface of the dream.

Henson clearly wanted to tell a particular story with the masquerade scene. "She knows that she's too young to be here," he says. "It's attractive, but also repellant."[50] Now we're getting to the root of fantasy: something we only dimly perceive, and might not even want, if we saw it in the light of day.

Henson's work has never portrayed romance in a straightforward way, if at all. In *The Muppets*, Miss Piggy is hopelessly obsessed with Kermit, who responds with a kind of infuriating affability, a chumminess that only further enrages her. *Can't he see that I'm in love with him?* Like Henson, Kermit is distracted by the show's production. He's just always working. In the documentary *Idea Man*, Frank Oz talks about how Miss Piggy's entire character is based upon insecurity. She knows that she's not as talented as the rest of the Muppets, and her claims to being a singer/actress are specious, at best. She can't run the show; she can't lead the band; she can't book the talent. But she can get laughs by karate-chopping Kermit at random moments. She's fat and loud and powerful — all the things a woman isn't supposed to be. Her desires are messy and visible at all times.

In the featurette, when Henson describes the masked ball as Sarah's fantasy, he specifies it as the experience of encountering an adult situation that we, as children, can't quite parse. In this way of thinking, we're meant to see an attraction bloom between Sarah and Jareth that is, possibly, a premonition of future crushes or relationships with older men. I've talked with many people who name the Goblin King as a kind of sexual

50 Ibid.

awakening for them, when they were too young to understand what the attraction meant. Still, I'm not sure I buy the idea that this is purely a romantic scenario, especially given that Henson's body of work suggests that straightforward romance was not his priority. Sarah is drawn to Jareth for a number of reasons that are not about love — his power, his fantastical world, his glamour — but she's still 14, and her stepmother notes that she isn't going on dates at all. Perhaps what's unsettling and intoxicating about this dance with Jareth is that it represents a crystallized version of her fantasy to escape the real world. She's literally locked in the amber of her dreams, and couldn't be any closer to getting what she wants.

But Sarah might not know what she wants at all. And whether she knows it or not, that's a state of being that will never truly go away.

## ILLUSIONS OF ROMANCE

Similarly, *The Dark Crystal* avoids anything like a traditional romance. The main characters, Kira and Jen, are too focused on their quest to really think about attraction (and who knows how Gelfling sexuality works — they could be in some wild polycule). The film's most memorable characters — the scientist Aughra, and SkekSil, the cloying Lord Chamberlain — are both solitary and more than a little off-putting. The Lord Chamberlain, once he's stripped of his armor, is full of voracious need, begging Jen for help. But Aughra is entirely

self-sufficient in her wonderous laboratory. Henson's work has always celebrated a delightful hag, and Aughra is perhaps the clearest embodiment of that figure. She's wise, sarcastic, and complete. She doesn't put up with any Gelfling bullshit. She's the eyes of her world, seeing everything, and nothing surprises her anymore. She wants you to leave so she can return to her giant telescope and her model of the solar system. Like Henson, she's always working, and work brings her a sense of peace that she can't find anywhere else. What she's not looking for is a date.

*Labyrinth* only presents us with one healthy relationship, and it's the worm at the start who lives with their "missus" and invites Sarah in for a cup of tea. Nothing in the film ever suggests that romance is a particularly compelling theme, so the eroticism of the ballroom scene feels all the more grotesque. It's the work of someone, I'd argue, who had profoundly ambivalent ideas about romance.[51] An idea clarified by Brian Henson, who says of his parents: "They were the love of each other's lives who couldn't live with each other."[52] Perhaps, for Henson, marriage was a masquerade in a crystal, a fascinating dream. But eventually, you had to break the glass.

I don't know if my parents were the love of each other's lives. They both found other people. I know my mother regrets

51 Interestingly, Henson had a reputation when he was younger as someone who dated quite a bit. It wasn't just distance that put a strain on his marriage. But it can be hard to reconcile this idea with the relationships he put on-screen, which were often more focused on kinship than traditional romance. He seems to have had a wry, even bawdy sense of humor when it came to sexuality, but he didn't care to portray physical romance in his stories.

52 *Labyrinth*, Blu-ray featurette.

their divorce, though at the time, my father was unable to be an equal partner in their marriage. He stopped working with her, and he withdrew into a space where his decisions were solitary. For years, he was unable to settle on a career that he found livable as a creative, playful idealist. Like Henson, my father has a refined sense of wonder, but at times, it has kept him from dealing with the grimy mechanics of the world. I think of that moment captured on camera, me in my Bowie shirt, crying or about to cry. I can smell the freshly cut grass, feel the yellow siding of our house on Lewis Street under my fingers, but I can't remember what I was feeling at the time.

*

In the early scene when Jareth shows Sarah his crystals, those famous hand tricks weren't actually performed by David Bowie — it was the artist Michael Moschen, crouched behind the actor. Even he could barely execute the trick, since he wasn't able to see what he was doing. It became an exercise in frustration. So really, the Goblin King offers Sarah something that's impossible to pull off, both in performance and in the world of the film. Jareth tempts Sarah with her own dreams. But what does he mean by this, exactly? Is it her dream of avoiding adult responsibility? Of staying in a fantasy world forever? Or is it a more complex dream that involves claiming power in her own life, being an individual, and not following heteronormative models? It could be a dream of agency, or a dream of forever staying the same. Part of Sarah's journey in

the film is listening to herself, not Jareth or her stepmother, and figuring out what she, deep down, might actually want.

If you gave me one wish, I wouldn't use it to bring peace to the world. I'd travel back to the Cottonwood Mall in 1986 and retrace my steps back to the toy store, where I once bought a mechanical snail during a time in my life when I felt safe and watched over. The air of the food court was blue with smoke, and I had no power to understand the maze of the social world, but I'd still go back there.

Sarah manages to pull off an impossible trick at the end of the film, an echo of the distressingly adult crystal ball dance. She doesn't get stuck in the junkyard of memory, but she still maintains a sense of childlike wonder. She needs her monsters, her goblins, and they return to her. She grows up, while holding on to beloved childhood things. We're all trying to do this, aren't we, even as we reach midlife and beyond?

Early in the film, Sarah tries to solve the doors with logic. But the maze only works on illogic and she ends up in the dangerous grasp of the "helping hands," who want to fix her while also tearing her apart. Henson seems to be suggesting not only that life is full of impossible, illogical choices, but that you still have to *choose*, even when it doesn't make sense. Even when it's not fair. But, at the same time, we shouldn't *have* to choose between childhood magic and a grayscale adult world. Can't we have both, if we're intentional about it? Can't we take the advice of the trash heap in *Fraggle Rock* and hold on to the magic? Invite the goblins into our home? One of our lifelong tasks is to radically redefine what it means to be

an "adult" in a world that has always been on fire, a world where it isn't always easy to reach for joy. The real choice isn't between childhood and adulthood — rather, it's the choice to intentionally become a *magical* adult.

There's a goblin in you that always tells the truth, and one that always lies. Is it annoying to say that they're the same?

Henson wants us to open all the doors. That's the point.

## NEURO-CHANGELINGS: MASQUERADES ON THE SPECTRUM

There may also be something deeper at work here — something that potentially resonates with autistic and otherwise neurodiverse readers. Being called "unconvincing" in the performance of your life is, often, a common experience for autistic kids who learn how to mask in order to suppress their authentic ways of being. "Masking" generally refers to behavior that brings someone in line with the expectations of being a sociable person under North America's particular blend of capitalism and ableism. This might include shaking hands; maintaining consistent eye contact; suppressing physical or auditory behaviors that might make you feel more at home in your body (stimming); engaging in very specific give-and-take dialogue with clear informational boundaries; interpreting complex gestures, body language, and irony; and always feeling like you "fit" into particular social and economic categories, like full-time employment and "usefulness." In *Unmasking Autism*, Devon

Price says that "before I started unmasking, I felt cursed . . . now, though life can still be difficult, I feel incredibly alive."[53]

But it's not always easy to take your mask off.

Growing up, I had particular issues with eye contact, body language, and understanding levels of sarcasm. I believed what people told me, however outlandish it might have been (once, at an embarrassingly older age, I believed a friend who said that Lionel Richie was hiding in their bathroom). I struggled with physical touch and was upset by loud noises and any unexpected stimuli. When I was six, and my mother came to pick me up from school, she asked why I wasn't playing with the other kids. *My brain works differently*, I said. She accepted this and handed me the crinkly gold paper from her Matinée Slims to play with. I was lucky to have a parent who didn't push me toward "correct" sociability, though I still had to do an exhausting amount of masking in order to get through the day. Now I do less. But I remember, vividly, the feeling that life would never make sense, because I hadn't received my basic instructions in the mail.

This brings me back to the idea of the changeling child. We see these stories in the earliest English medieval tradition: a fairy steals someone's newborn, and replaces them with a changeling. They look the same, but their actions are peculiar, alien. The parents desperately try to recover their original child, sometimes making reckless bargains with the fae. It's worth noting, as well, that goblins belong to this category of

53 Price, Introduction, ebook.

supernatural being. Like fairies, they can be household spirits, or forest-dwellers, often chaotic in their behavior. In fact, in *Outside Over There*, the goblins swap Ida's baby brother for one of their own. But he's not quite a goblin — he's described as a changeling. Ida finds him to be cold, unresponsive, and in one unsettling illustration by Sendak, we see him melting like a block of ice.

Changelings are often seen as poorly made versions of the original child, as if the fairies had fashioned them out of rag, ice, and shadow. Like normal children, but conspicuously off in every way (one changeling in a Scottish myth looks like the farmer's son, but keeps rising toward the ceiling or breaking through the walls of the house — he doesn't understand his own power). The goal is always to return the changeling to their proper realm, and never to understand them on their own terms. You don't learn to love the changeling: you exchange them for the child you *really* want. And if this is sounding like the tone of many "Autism moms" who post on social media or publish saintly, self-aggrandizing memoirs, that's no coincidence. The ancient story of the changeling can be laid, with surprising ease, over the experience of contemporary neurodiverse kids who can't fulfill their parents' expectations of "normal" sociability.

Author Sarah Kurchak, in her comedic memoir *I Overcame My Autism*, describes how she felt like a changeling and a cuckoo child — terrified by the idea that she might not be a real person. This childhood fear is remarkably uniform among neurodiverse adults that I've spoken with: the sense that you

were only pretending to be real, and everyone could always tell. But maybe, if you masked hard enough, your family wouldn't try to exchange you for an easier child. Someone they recognized, instead of the changeling, the black sheep, the android, or the goblin that you could feel under your skin, ruining everything.

*Labyrinth* retells the changeling myth, and it also reframes Sendak's story, by crafting Sarah as a more complex heroine. She doesn't necessarily like her baby brother. She clashes with her stepmother, and she feels disappointed in her father. She straddles boundaries and refuses to change. She's smart, sometimes petulant, often angry. She puts on medieval mystery plays in the park instead of hanging out with kids her age. When a seductive immortal flies through her window in the form of an owl, she looks more annoyed than frightened.

I connected with Sarah at an early age because, like me, she didn't quite fit into any of the narratives placed before her. And the reviewers who criticized Connelly's performance were also, in a way, criticizing their understanding of what it meant to be a clever teenage girl. *We don't recognize this girl*, they were effectively saying. *This is an unconvincing performance — not a real person*. And I'd argue that most neurodiverse kids would understand this blow against their subjectivity, because they've been told some version of this from an early age. *You say you're human, but we don't believe you. What fairy realm did you come from?* Even if reviews of her performance were casually negative, we can also see them as a misunderstanding of Connelly's version of Sarah. Siskel and the others wanted a likeable Molly Ringwald, but what they got was a prickly girl who dances

In many ways — and like many kids — Sarah has found shelter in the liberatory space of her dreams. She's done so even at the expense of forming connections with other humans. When Jareth offers Sarah her dreams, what he seems to be giving her is something comfortable, something that comes from within her own fantasy world. But if we follow our dreams to the detriment of our own messy development, we're also producing a cruel optimism: the flawed idea that if we cling to familiar, unchanging fantasy, then our lives will somehow make sense. Magic, as Henson has always said, should be a guiding force within our lives. We shouldn't relinquish our dreams because the world throws up brick walls. But we also can't hold onto a *particular* dream without letting it transform — especially if it's holding us back. Even if it wears a feather cloak and sexily assures us that this whole thing isn't about control.

*Labyrinth* has always been about the complexity of a teen girl's power. But it remains unclear who actually lives within whom, if that's how we want to define it. Sarah's triumph over the Goblin King — her insistence that he's never had power over her — suggests that the world of the labyrinth has always been inside her mind. She created Jareth and his goblins, and she has the power to dismiss them. But is that the case? Yes, all of the goblins exist in her bedroom, in one form or another, and she reads from a book that seems to encapsulate the film's plot. We could see all of this as a literary daydream that becomes a nightmare.

But the goblins appear in Sarah's bedroom afterward, when she calls upon them, as the viewer watches Jareth fly

away in owl form. There's a collision of worlds, and it's not entirely clear what Henson wants us to take from this. Do the goblins dance in her bedroom because they're a part of her childhood that she refuses to give up, yet has somehow transformed? Is this still a kind of daydream? Or are there real, flesh-and-blood goblins in her room, just as they appeared earlier, to snatch away her little brother? The crux of the film is the question of whether Sarah's journey has been real or psychological, to the extent that we can even fully separate those two experiences.

Brian Froud didn't care for the ending with the bedroom dance party. He found it to be too campy. But Henson insisted, and we have to assume that he held onto this ambivalence for a reason. Sarah takes the magic of the labyrinth — the magic of childhood — back to the "real" world. We can't really say that the labyrinth itself, whether it's a dream or not, has been any less real than her experience as a suburban teen. *Labyrinth* collapses both worlds, in order to show us how close they are to one another. Our personal labyrinths hold all of these contradictions, from childhood wonder to the crucial unfairness of being an adult. Everything can fit in this miraculous engine, where we'll never run out of twists and turns.

Sarah's power doesn't simply emerge from the fact that this has all been a dream. That would be too easy, and not in keeping with Henson's love of ambiguity. Instead, her power comes from knowing that nothing is simple. There will never be fair answers, but there will always be choices. She has the power to reject domination, and the power to retain what's

joyful about her childhood. She can hold onto magic, and dance with it, even if she's the only one who sees it. She doesn't need Jareth to rule her, because she can make her own decisions and create her own worlds.

That may be the greatest gift of the film: it points us toward world-building. It shows us that, like Sarah, we can feel amazed by the worlds that we create. We can dance, fearlessly, on the edge of our own dreams.

# 7

## Nostalgia and *Labyrinth's* Afterlives

People still talk about *Labyrinth* nearly 40 years after its release, which is particularly impressive when we consider that 1986 also gave us *Top Gun*, *Ferris Bueller's Day Off*, and *Aliens*. This was a banner year for eighties fantasy cinema, and though *Labyrinth* hasn't yet had a reboot like *Top Gun*, I'd argue that we have much stronger feelings about Henson's cult classic than we do about That Volleyball Scene. *Top Gun* is a film that focuses, almost entirely, on men having *feelings* about other men. The shirtless beach volleyball game is meant to show off their perfect American physiques, but it also conveys the message of many films from this era: *these guys should probably fuck*. Or at least admit that they might care about each other. So much of specifically eighties homophobia involves men being unable to imagine tenderness, while ruthlessly

hunting/stalking/devastating each other. *Labyrinth* offers something much less expected. And, frankly, it's aged better.

Though *Dark Crystal* was the more commercially successful film at the outset, it doesn't quite provoke the sentiment that we feel for *Labyrinth*. The film has produced video games, tarot decks, multiple DVD sets with special features, masquerade parties, midnight viewings, music videos, and the potential for both a cinematic reboot and a stage show.[54] We remember the darker elements of the story, but, as with all of Henson's work, there's a spirit of play that endures. Whenever I mention *Labyrinth* to anyone between the ages of 30 and 45, they almost immediately begin to sing "Magic Dance." Bowie's rough velvet voice, the joyful lyrics, and the paradox of a baby laughing surrounded by goblins have all served to encode the song in our collective DNA.

But it's also specifically of its time, in spite of the fantasy. The pre-CGI owl, the synth pop, the suburban teen looking for adventure: they're like fingerprints for 1986. Writing this book has allowed me to time travel back to that era, but it's also reminded me of the impossibility of going backward. Sarah's sweet deal — *have your adulthood, and the goblins too* — isn't a spell that most of us can master, living under time and capitalism. Is it possible to trap yourself in the amber of childhood and never come back? Stephen Hawking said that traveling to the past was impossible, but we might be able to go into

54 Recently, it was officially announced that Robert Eggers would direct a sequel — I can only imagine how the director of *Nosferatu* will handle the story.

the future.[55] As a writer, this feels like a bad deal; the future is anxious enough, without my presence. Instead, what we want is a magnifying glass for the past.

By 1986, the AIDS crisis was raging across the United States and Canada, with an average of 5,000 people dying every year. Queer and trans people, along with their straight friends, were attending funerals each week. In *How to Survive a Plague*, David France notes that Reagan actually *reduced* funding to AIDS research in 1986, "including a $29 million cut in treatment."[56] This was after Rock Hudson's public death, and in spite of a bill that had recently passed in New York, protecting the employment and housing rights of people with AIDS. Mainstream cinema had very little to say about what was essentially a government-sanctioned pandemic. Aside from a few independent films like *Parting Glances* (with a young Steve Buscemi), the box office was more concerned with big adventure films. It was still distressingly common to hear homophobic slurs in mainstream comedy films, and to see audiences laugh at stereotyped gay men on-screen.

We were experiencing an onslaught of casual rage and disgust directed at queer people who were dying at a horrific rate, with a few flashes of radical counter-comedy. In his 2002 book, *Melancholia and Moralism*, AIDS activist Douglas Crimp observes that "much has changed" since his early AIDS writing, "but then again, much has remained the same . . . Sometimes

55 Sutter, "Stephen Hawking's Time Travel Party."

56 France, 217.

the déjà vu seems more like a nightmare from which we cannot awaken."[57] I felt this more than ever in January of 2025, when Trump declared that America would only "recognize" two genders. How swiftly we can be written out of existence as queer and trans people. But instead, I see the battle within the Goblin City. We're scraps of blue and green, facing down the hollow puppet Humongous. Even Hoggle swings an axe to protect his friends. This labyrinth is ours, and always has been.

Henson worked with multiple queer people and would have understood what was happening within his extended arts community, even if he didn't necessarily talk about it. Richard Hunt, the puppeteer who'd first joined him on *Sesame Street*, was openly gay. He'd flirted with Rudolf Nureyev on the set of *The Muppet Show* and added a dash of queer humor to characters like Gladys the Cow (whom pop culture scholar Matt Baume describes as a drag queen in his book *Hi Honey, I'm Homo!*). When Hunt was dying of AIDS, his co-worker Frank Oz sat by his bedside. After all, Hunt performed the eulogy at Henson's funeral. Unlike so many people, Hunt didn't perish alone.

Henson's work has always championed the importance of love, kindness, and care. And while *Labyrinth* does dramatize what seems like a fairy-tale love story, it's virtually impossible not to read the whole story as queer in tone. Sarah has no interest in dating anyone. Her bedroom is full of books by Maurice Sendak rather than band posters. Yes, she does

57 Crimp, 17.

enter into an unsettling relationship with an immortal goblin who can take any shape he pleases, but the film ends with a repudiation of servitude and control, rather than a swooning kiss, as we see in a film like *Legend* from just one year earlier. Henson's stories have never prioritized romance, and this is one reason that I appreciated them as a younger viewer. The rest of cinema was telling me that I needed to get muscular, wear a tank top, and flirt with a quiet girl who laughed at all my jokes. And while counter-films like *Heathers* tried to pry apart this fantasy, the message was persistent. Henson's films were much more interested in creating non-traditional relationships. Sarah ends the film in a kind of platonic polycule with several goblins, a squirrel knight, a dancing fire fairy, and a friendly beast who could actually tear the roof off her home. She's seen as complete without having to be in any type of traditional relationship, and we're even urged to sympathize with her stepmother, who doesn't want to be seen as wicked. *Labyrinth* remains a film that's queer down to its very roots, even if not every audience member clues in.

## *LABYRINTH* AND GAMING

There were two game adaptations of *Labyrinth* that I was eager to try — one for the Commodore 64, and one for Nintendo that was only released in Japan. *Labyrinth* did quite well in Japan, which suggests that Henson's world might have been more compatible with the surging anime culture of

the eighties. Alongside anime titles like *Macross*, *Bubblegum Crisis*, and the lighter *Dirty Pair*, Henson's goblin tale blurred the lines between slapstick comedy and existential themes. *Labyrinth: The Computer Game* represented Lucasfilm's first foray into PC games, which placed a fair bit of pressure on the enterprise. It used "word wheels" instead of the standard text parser that we'd see in games like *King's Quest*, and this early interface would go on to influence the enormously popular point-and-click adventure games of the nineties. As with the film, the game was perhaps slightly ahead of its time, but it enjoyed a reasonable commercial success.

As a player, you begin by answering some questions about yourself, including your sex. There's no way to avoid this. If you type "unknown," the game actually replies with *I doubt that's true*. It's fascinating to me how the game anticipates that you might try to avoid the gender binary. The response is a light joke, and there's literally no way out of the exchange without choosing M or F — but there's still a kind of sly subversion to the way it was programmed. *We know you're there, gender nonconformists. But we've got a limited number of sprites to choose from — sorry.* Even later PC games didn't often give you a choice in this regard, since the default player was always male. It's as if the game wants to acknowledge its own limitations, which feels almost charming, in spite of the essentialism.

Is *Labyrinth: The Computer Game* a masterpiece of ambivalent storytelling, like the film on which it was based? I think we all know the answer to this. The game is basic and clunky, though I was delighted to hear a MIDI version of "Within

You" blaring as a kind of tinny crescendo. Your character goes to a movie theater, presumably to watch *Labyrinth*, though the actual film is never named. You get into an argument with a film nerd — literally described as wearing "glasses and a pocket protector" — who won't stop talking about how much he loves the film. I'll admit: I was enchanted by this naked capitalist tie-in. The idea of the video game directly promoting the movie — by having your character watch the film in-game — felt like a much more contemporary use of marketing meta-text.

Of course, the game/film is interrupted by Jareth, who appears on the screen in 16 glorious colors. His hair is an unnatural shade of gold, as if he'd dyed it mere seconds ago. *We've been watching you*, he says. *We know everything, including your weaknesses.* In spite of the fact that sci-fi author Douglas Adams did some work on the game, it loses all of the nuanced dialogue of the film. Jareth sounds more like a villain from *Zork* than a seductive sorcerer. Though Adams did insist on adding the word *adumbrate* to the text system, which means a kind of foreshadowing. There's still a shadow of linguistic play that survives when you have to *adumbrate* an elephant, in order to break out of the locked oubliette. There's a sense of whimsy in these older games that's harder to capture now, with the photorealistic graphics of blockbuster titles like *Diablo* and *Baldur's Gate*, a gentle shrug at the game's limitations, and a callback to the text-based systems that allowed in-jokes and creative solutions in the absence of staggering visuals.

The second game, released only in Japan, was called *Maze of the Goblin King*. My boyfriend downloaded this with an emulator, and we attempted to play it. The game has an early *Legend of Zelda* feel, and I was surprised that it roughly followed the plot of the film. You can chat with major characters, and Jareth appears to taunt you at several moments. Granted, he sounds like a *Sailor Moon* villain, but it's hard to translate Bowie's wit and sex appeal into a game that mostly involves throwing rocks at fairies. The fairies were such a small part of the film that it seemed odd to focus on them as the primary antagonists. But there's something sly about this, as well. It captures the film's way of upending fairy tales or, rather, digging into the depths of their wild ambiguity. When a beautiful fairy bites Sarah in the film, Hoggle responds: *What do you expect fairies to do?* Sarah protests that they're supposed to do nice things. Hoggle laughs: *Shows what you know.* These fairies are a radical departure from the helpful sprites we'll see in virtually all future *Zelda* games. Everything in the labyrinth ranges from a kind of pest to something that might eat you. I was particularly enchanted by the idea of the worm as a friendly shopkeeper. Since the worm famously misdirects Sarah in the film, having them sell you items feels like a bit of wry humor.

It was also delightfully odd to have a character throwing rocks instead of wielding a sword. The game preserves Henson's use of whimsical violence and avoids the more standard medievalist combat system that would establish such a choke hold on later Nintendo games. Did we get far? No. Watching Sarah

throw rocks was not engrossing. But I was surprised by the detail of adaptation and wondered what *Maze of the Goblin King* would have looked like as a more sophisticated adventure game.

Of all the *Labyrinth* adaptations — including a sweet board game and a graphic novel series — why am I talking about two outdated games? The short answer is that these early adaptations reveal a particular style of tie-in that reared its head in the eighties, then never sank back into the depths. It became the model for consuming fantasy media at the time. *Dungeons & Dragons* inspired new campaigns, which created fantasy novel tie-ins like *Dragonlance* and *Forgotten Realms*, which led to PC games, and on and on. We sometimes think of current blockbuster marketing as a monster of the digital era, but it began in the eighties, when most North American neoliberal structures crystallized like some kind of awful, capitalist ice sculpture. Why just read a book, when you could play a game, watch a film, and discover a comic tie-in? In 1986, it was already possible to play the Commodore 64 *Labyrinth* game while reading the comic and listening to the soundtrack on cassette tape.

This media attack runs counter to Henson's deep storytelling practices, which often mingle humor with philosophy and critique. But we can't forget that Henson also launched involved media tours for both *Labyrinth* and *The Dark Crystal*, and he eventually sold the rights to *The Muppets* — a paradoxical move, considering how hard he worked to initially buy back the rights to other properties. He saw Disney as a good home for his many worlds — a secure landing pad — though it's unclear whether he could have imagined the monster that Disney would become.

Like Humongous — the machine who guards the entrance to the Goblin City — they would swing their battle axe in a wide arc over the next three decades. Now it's hard to imagine something they don't own. *The Rocky Horror Picture Show* — one of the best-known radical queer and anti-establishment films ever made — is now streaming on Disney, for example.

Henson wanted a home for the Muppets; he didn't want Disney to *own* them. But these decisions are never simple. Like growing up, you have to make cursed choices while still holding on to some magic.

## MAZES OF NOSTALGIA

I've also chosen these weird little games because of an idea that structures this weird little book: *nostalgia*. Translated literally, it means "homesickness" but also "the pain of returning home." Working on this book has immersed me in nostalgia, even when I was trying to avoid it by somehow staying objective. One of my students, when asked about the film, wondered if it would still hold up. It reminded me of rewatching *Labyrinth* as a grad student, through the haze of wine and academic dread. We were all looking for something in the film — a reversible door back to our childhoods. But you can't step into the same Bog of Eternal Stench twice. Nothing could equal my theatrical encounter with *Labyrinth* as an eight-year-old, because it was a wild moment in time, as irrecoverable as Jennifer Connelly's teenage enthusiasm for all those stunts and messy sequences.

I've rewatched the film in my twenties, thirties, and forties, and it's resonated differently each time. Now, perhaps distressingly, I empathize with Sarah's beleaguered parents, who just want a night away from their toddler. *We go out so rarely*, her stepmother says. After ignoring her father's (admittedly mild) attempts at reconciliation, Sarah yells back sarcastically: *You really wanted to talk to me, didn't you? Practically broke down the door!* As teen rebellions go, handing off your baby brother to goblins does feel a bit dramatic. And if your kid showed up late and dripping wet on the single night you'd chosen to escape your adult responsibilities for a few hours, wouldn't you be annoyed? Might you not wish they'd take up smoking, or going on mediocre dates, instead of LARPing in a public park and treating you like a cinematic villain?

By the standards of a contemporary film like *The Breakfast Club*, Sarah feels a bit archaic, a bit innocent. She's out of time in the same way that Henson's work often defies popular conventions, opting instead for ideas like friendship and love that would have seemed cringeworthy to most eighties teens. *You should have dates at your age*, her stepmother says, a bit wistfully. What I've always appreciated about this scene is that there's no mention of boys in particular. *Dates* feels like a wide-open concept, even if we know that it was probably shorthand for guys who looked like Duckie from *Pretty in Pink*. Sarah doesn't seem to be hitting any of the psychological milestones that we used to see reflected in after school specials and other media for teens of the era. She's holding on to that gossamer

boundary between childhood and adulthood in a way that feels almost uncomfortably relatable to me.

As a closeted queer teen who came of age in the eighties and nineties, I saw no reflection of my desires on-screen, save for occasional characters who quipped and then vanished (like a drive-by gay joke in an otherwise straight narrative). Before *The Birdcage* in 1996, I'd never seen a positive depiction of a queer relationship. It wasn't safe for me to even accidentally brush a boy's fingertips, and the thought of kissing — or more — was unimaginable. I watched other kids break into pairs, those shaky middle-school relationships that involved more passing of notes than actual making out, and it felt like watching a foreign film without subtitles. After I came out in my late teens, I assumed this delayed track would fix itself. But autism turned out to be the surprising sequel, my version of *Gremlins II: The New Batch* (which is fair, since I also love eating after midnight and hate getting wet). Sarah resonates with me in a very particular way, because we were both judged for our childish qualities. The problem was that she was able to mystically unite those two worlds, and I still got flack during dates for wanting to analyze the queer complexity of Ursula from *The Little Mermaid*.

*

As I get older, the character from *Labyrinth* that I appreciate most is the junk lady. After Sarah breaks out of the crystal ball

masquerade, she lands in a postapocalyptic junk heap. Shadowy figures shuffle around her, dragging things with them, but we can't quite make them out. It's like something out of *The Dark Crystal*, but it feels even more unsettling, because there's something very real about this hazy nightmare trash heap. One of the figures yells: *Get off my back!* And we discover that Sarah has been crouching on top of an old creature: a scowling woman who carries an assortment of broken items on her shoulders. There are chairs and busted toys and unidentifiable fragments. In the *Labyrinth* featurette, Brian Henson talks about how he also learned to appreciate the simple but brilliant metaphor that his father had crafted with the junk lady. "As we get older, we carry all of this baggage on our backs." The puppet itself was deviously complicated, and even seasoned puppeteer Karen Prell had a difficult time with it. She had to shuffle around in the dark, her face concealed by the junk, while animating the woman's sly, expressive face with her hand. It sounds a lot like growing up: wading through garbage and the detritus of memory, unable to see more than a few inches in front of your face, and even that's just an outline.

In his article on overconsumption in the film, David Burns argues that *Labyrinth* reflects Henson's lifelong focus on environmentalism: "The junk lady's pile of junk is an impermeable physical border of discarded consumer goods . . . [her] reflection in the mirror foretells Sarah's future life if she continues valuing consumer goods over relationships."[58] Henson's other projects,

58 Burns, "Overconsumption and Environmentalism in *Labyrinth*," 50.

like *Fraggle Rock*, also deal with ecology, and songs like "Bein' Green" celebrate the vibrancy of nature. But in spite of Sarah's conspicuous consumption, I'm not convinced that the message is one of valuing toys over relationships. What the junk lady offers Sarah is her childhood, visualized through toys and books and a music box that we assume was a gift from her mother. The ultimate temptation is for her to simply return to being a child, without the anxiety of having to save her baby brother from the Goblin King. But Sarah chooses to go forward, and watching the film as adults, we're offered a similar choice. We know that it's impossible to go back. Yet we still need those childish things, and Henson makes sure we know that it's okay to reach for old memories, old stories.

"I didn't like the ending," Brian Froud says in the director's commentary, "with the party. I cringe at it. But Jim insisted."[59] There's a shot of Sir Didymus in a party hat, clearly having the time of his life. Even the cranky old sage with a bird demon on his head is dancing and throwing confetti. It always makes me think of a goblin gay bar: everyone gets to try on different versions of themselves. Nostalgia may be part of the film's magic, but we're not meant to either reject it or see through it.

Instead, we put on a party hat, and dance with it.

59 *Labyrinth* DVD commentary by Brian Froud.

The mid-sized campus where I teach is a labyrinth of its own. It seemed small when I first moved here, since my experience was with bigger universities. But as I walked from my office at one end of campus, to a colleague's office all the way on the other side, I could feel the baffling turns, the corners and hidden staircases. I've been running through this particular campus maze for 15 years now, but I rarely just allow myself to wander. Once, I discovered an outside corner with flowering trees and a bench. Often, I've found myself reading beneath a large painting of Christ in the library of the Catholic college, which is not something I ever expected to do when I was studying queer theory on a mountain in Vancouver. (I guess Jesus and I both relate to mountains, at least.) My colleague's office had toy versions of Sendak's wild things, and I couldn't help but talk about this book. *I always loved the magic dance*, they said, offering me a mug of apple cider. We talked about queer community and nonbinary b'mitzvahs, and joked with our friend about the perils of dating in Regina. I laughed about a failed threesome. This was queer community in a small city.

We talked about the individual mazes of desire and duty and learning that had led us to this prairie university, where we complained every day about the weather. Some of us had loves in different cities. All of us, in one way or another, felt torn between different lives, even as we tried to maintain grooves here. A *multicursal* labyrinth has individual chambers, like a heart, and it can lead you to surprising corners. In her book

*Red Thread*, Charlotte Higgins talks about visiting the outskirts of Knossos, where the myth of the labyrinth supposedly began. Years later, she returned to a correspondence with her tour guide from that time, who wrote back: "To be inside a maze or a labyrinth is to be bewildered, confused, or afraid . . . but only up to a point. It is also to be held within a design or a pattern."[60] If we build our labyrinths, then we can solve them. And in the meantime, they hold us, through life's always-surprising bifurcations.

So often, when I mention *Labyrinth* to someone, they grin and say *magic dance*. My friend's son went through a period of dancing in the basement for exercise, as if he was Max from *Where the Wild Things Are*. I used to dance until 3 a.m. at Luvafair and The Odyssey in Vancouver, then devour a slice of 99-cent pizza. I'd write until dawn, grab a coffee, and teach a class. I was feral and could barely communicate with my peers, but time seemed under my control. My 20-something body could climb endless flights of stairs, have sex on futons, and collapse, laughing, in a bowling alley parking lot, after giving drunken piggy-back rides. Like Sarah, I still thought fairies did nice things. I thought academia had my best interests at heart, even though we were told that if we couldn't find tenure-track jobs in our field, *the profession might not be for you*.

When I watch *Labyrinth* at age 45, I see all those ghostly versions of me, wandering. The eight-year-old who sang "As the World Falls Down" until it actually did. The 18-year-old

60 Higgins, 9.

who held a boy's hand while watching *Titanic* at the same theater — now gone — where *Labyrinth* had first enchanted. The 30-year-old typing *autism diagnosis* into a search bar, then curling up on the floor next to the cat. And whoever I am now. A child of forever, hanging Christmas decorations from *My Neighbor Totoro* on a Charlie Brown–sized tree, while our cat forgets that she's a senior and leaps on the garland.

In her poem "I Have a Time Machine," Brenda Shaughnessy says: "The past is so horribly fast."[61] We're all piloting our labyrinths across space and time, watching in disbelief as David Bowie charms the clock forward.

Henson worried so often about time. How there wasn't enough of it. His heart was a beating clock, and he hurled art into the world with a sense of urgency. In *Fraggle Rock*, Marjory the Trash Heap teaches us the most important lesson: *You cannot leave the magic*. You take it with you, wherever you go, like childhood.

Jareth laughs when we tell him it's not fair.

It still feels like an impossible trick. How do we maintain our childhood sense of the miraculous while stumbling through the adult world? How can we float up impossible staircases and still file our taxes on time? As Jareth tries to teach us: it's not about the unfairness of things. It's about telling a story both foul and fair. A text that weaves both of those threads — child and adult — together. Life isn't fair. Of course it's not. Life is the magic dance and life is the knowledge that you'll lose

61 Shaughnessy, "I Have a Time Machine," Prelude.

someone forever. We can't always look back and see a clear, intentional path. But that doesn't mean we aren't progressing.

*

In the introduction, I talked about the spectacle of *Labyrinth*. What needful thing did it offer at the time? Why was its song of transformation so powerful?

It taught me to see life as a puzzle, complete with frustration and delight. As a queer and neurodiverse kid, I felt like the pains of life overwhelmed the pleasures. Everything was hard and bright and wrong and confusing. I was Sarah falling down the pit full of helping hands, and none of them helped, they all just flung me around. But *Labyrinth* gave me glorious possibilities, and I think it's still doing that, particularly for those who are queer and neurodiverse. It showed me that the puzzle was the point, that life could be riddling, but it was the experience that mattered, not the solution. Henson wanted to show kids that they were powerful, that they could stand up to tyranny, even if the monster was of their own design. Even if *they* were the monsters, that was fine too, because we're all monstrous, at least sometimes.

Like Ludo, we don't know our own strength. Like Hoggle, we can run from our responsibilities. Like Sir Didymus, we can get stuck in our own patterns and forget to ask the most important questions. Like Jareth, we can sulk and fritter away our own potential while trying to live in an imaginary throne room.

Sarah is a hero and a monster and a girl. She wants to grow up, and she also wants to stay a kid, and maybe she even wants some impossible in-between space. The important thing is that she *wants*, and she doesn't apologize for that. She has her goblins, and dances with them too. Like Henson, she insists upon the weird ending, the neither this nor that, because life doesn't have to be about the disappointments of growing up. It can be an eternally awkward party, where we leap from ecstasy to catastrophe, never knowing what's around the next hedge.

My campus is currently shrouded in construction, so that no path is the same each day. We're always being diverted and surprised. A staircase might function one week, and then be cordoned off the next. We're blazing new neuronal paths, taking strange twists and turns. I joke with a friend about writing this book, and how our workplace has also become a labyrinth. We're stumbling through middle age together, amazed by the journey. There are dead ends and trick doors, but also strange fire exits, submerged steps, and dreamy ballrooms. We joke about mortality. I ask her how it feels to turn 50, and she replies: *Closer to the grave*. I say: *It might be nice to become a wavelength*. We take the wrong stairs, and laugh. The goal is always just in sight, but we've forgotten it. Maybe that's the point. To meet the sharp edges of life with wonder. To share your labyrinth with someone who understands.

We don't have to leave the magic. We can refuse the choice, or make a new choice of our own invention. The ending to *Labyrinth* taught me to look forward to a wild goblin rumpus, a life of confetti and tragedy and amazement. Our lives are

labyrinths, and we should peer around every corner. We should fear the open spaces, but not too much, and love the dead ends for what they show us.

It might not be perfect. But it's only forever.

# Sources


Austen, Jane. *Pride and Prejudice*. Edited by Robert Irvine. Broadview, 2020.

Beagle, Peter S. *The Last Unicorn*. Ace, 1991.

Berlant, Lauren. *Cruel Optimism*. Duke University Press, 2011.

Block, Paula M. *Labyrinth: The Ultimate Visual History*. Insight Editions, 2016.

von Boehn, Max. *Puppets and Automata*. Dover, 1972.

Borges, Jorge Luis. *Ficciones*. Alianza Editorial, 2003.

Bray, Alan. *Homosexuality in Renaissance England*. Columbia University Press, 1996.

Burnett, Frances Hodgson. *The Secret Garden*. Edited by Shelley King and Heather K. Cyr. Broadview, 2024.

Burns, David R., and Deborah R. Burns. "Overconsumption and Environmentalism in *Labyrinth*." Chap. 5 in *Jim Henson and Philosophy: Imagination and the Magic of Mayhem*, edited by Timothy M. Dale and Joseph J. Foy. Rowan & Littlefield, 2015.

Butler, Judith. *Undoing Gender*. Routledge, 2004.

Butler, Judith. *Who's Afraid of Gender?* Picador, 2025.

Carroll, Lewis. *Alice's Adventures in Wonderland*. Edited by Richard Kelly. Broadview, 2011.

Carson, Anne. *Eros the Bittersweet*. Princeton Classics, 2023.

Castle, Terry. *Masquerade and Civilization*. Stanford University Press, 1986.

Cavafy, C.P. *Complete Poems*. Edited and translated by Daniel Mendelsohn. Knopf, 2012.

Clarke Gray, Brenna. "On Machine Learning and Academic Integrity." *Little EdTech, Big Mouth*, March 15, 2023.

Cleland, John. *Memoirs of a Woman of Pleasure*. Edited by Richard Terry and Helen Williams. Broadview, 2018.

Coyle, McKayla. *Goblin Mode: How to Get Cozy, Embrace Imperfection, and Thrive in the Muck*. Quirk Books, 2023.

Crimp, Douglas. *Melancholia and Moralism: Essays on AIDS and Queer Politics*. MIT Press, 2002.

Darnton, Nina. "Jim Henson's *Labyrinth*." *The New York Times*, June 27, 1986.

Donaldson, Kayleigh. "How *Labyrinth's* Fandom Is Stronger Than Ever After Its 35 Years." *IGN*, July 31, 2021.

Doob, Penelope. *The Idea of the Labyrinth: From Classical Antiquity Through the Middle Ages*. Cornell University Press, 1990.

Duane, Diane. *So You Want to Be a Wizard*. HarperCollins, 2001.

Ende, Michael. *Die unendliche Geshichte*. Thienemann, 2019.

France, David. *How to Survive a Plague: The Inside Story of How Citizens and Science Tamed AIDS*. Knopf, 2016.

Froud, Brian. *The Goblins of Labyrinth*. Abrams, 2006.

Ftacek, Julia. "Jonathan Swift and the Transgender Classroom." *Journal for Eighteenth-Century Studies* 43, no. 3, 2020, pp. 304–314.

Gay, Roxane. *Bad Feminist: Essays*. Harper Perennial, 2014.

Grimm, Jacob. *Selected Tales*. Edited by Joyce Crick. Oxford World's Classics, 2009.

Grimm, Jacob. *Teutonic Mythology, Volumes 1–4*. Edited and translated by James Stallybrass. Dover, 1966.

Halberstam, Jack. *The Queer Art of Failure*. Duke University Press, 2011.

Halberstam, Jack. *In a Queer Time and Place: Transgender Bodies, Subcultural Lives*. New York University Press, 2005.

Higgins, Charlotte. *Red Thread: On Mazes & Labyrinths*. Jonathan Cape, 2018.

Hoffmann, E.T.A. *Nutcracker*. Translated by Ralph Manheim. Illustrated by Maurice Sendak. Crown Publishers, 1984.

Jones, Brian Jay. *Jim Henson: The Biography*. Ballantine, 2016.

Jurkowski, Henryk. *A History of European Puppetry*. Edwin Mellen Press, 1998.

Knowles, John. *A Separate Peace*. Scribner, 2003.

Kurchak, Sarah. *I Overcame My Autism and All I Got Was This Lousy Anxiety Disorder: A Memoir*. Douglas & McIntyre, 2020.

Kurchak, Sarah. "Real Autism." *Hazlitt*, April 9, 2018.

Larrington, Carolyne. *King Arthur's Enchantresses*. I.B. Tauris, 2015.

MacDonald, George. *The Princess and the Goblin*. Penguin Young Readers, 2011.

Marlowe, Christopher. *Edward II*. Edited by Mathew R. Martin. Broadview, 2010.

Norton, Rictor. *Mother Clap's Molly House: The Gay Subculture in England 1700–1830*. Heretic Books, 1992.

Nussbaum, Martha. *Love's Knowledge: Essays on Philosophy and Literature*. Oxford University Press, 1992.

Perrault, Charles. *The Complete Fairy Tales*. Edited by Christopher Betts. Oxford World's Classics, 2010.

Pratchett, Terry. *The Wee Free Men*. Clarion Books, 2015.

Price, Devon. *Unmasking Autism: Discovering the New Faces of Neurodiversity*. Harmony, 2022.

Prince, Stephen, and Melissa Risley, editors. *American Cinema of the 1980s*. Rutgers University, 2007.

Prince, Stephen. "Genres and Production Cycles." Chap. 7 in *A New Pot of Gold: Hollywood Under the Electronic Rainbow, 1980–1989*. University of California Press, 2000.

Purdham, Adelle. *I Don't Do Disability and Other Lies I've Told Myself*. Dundurn, 2024.

Robberson, Joe. "Twenty Things You Never Knew About *Labyrinth*." *Zimbio*, January 20, 2016.

Rossetti, Christina. *Goblin Market*. Illustrated by Arthur Rackham. Dover, 2010.

Rossinow, Doug. *The Reagan Era: A History of the 1980s*. Columbia University Press, 2015.

de Saint-Exupéry, Antoine. *The Little Prince*. Translator: Richard Howard. Clarion, 2000.

Schulman, Sarah. *My American History: Lesbian and Gay Life During the Reagan and Bush Years*. Routledge, 1994.

Sendak, Maurice. *Outside Over There*. Harper & Row, 1981.

Sendak, Maurice. *Where the Wild Things Are*. HarperCollins, 2012.

Shakespeare, William. *A Midsummer Night's Dream*. Edited by Grace Ioppolo. W.W. Norton, 2018.

Shaughnessy, Brenda. "I Have a Time Machine." In *So Much Synth*. Copper Canyon, 2016.

Siskel, Gene. "Jim Henson's Wizardry Lost in *Labyrinth*." *The Chicago Tribune*, June 30, 1986.

Sookfong Lee, Jen. *Gentlemen of the Shade: My Own Private Idaho*. ECW, 2017.

Stine, Alison. "*Labyrinth* and the Dark Heart of Childhood." *Atlantic*, June 29, 2016.

Sutter, Paul. "Stephen Hawking's Time Travel Party." *Discover*, December 1, 2023.

Thom, Kai Cheng. *I Hope We Choose Love*. Arsenal Pulp Press, 2019.

Tolkien, J.R.R. *The Hobbit*. Houghton Mifflin, 2012.

Tolkein, J.R.R. *The Monsters and the Critics and Other Essays*. HarperCollins, 2013.

Walker, Nick. *Neuroqueer Heresies: Notes on the Neurodiversity Paradigm, Autistic Empowerment, and Postnormal Possibilities*. Autonomous Press, 2021.

Weis, Margaret, and Tracy Hickman. *Dragons of Autumn Twilight*. Wizards of the Coast, 2000.

White, T.H. *The Sword in the Stone*. HarperCollins, 2008.

Winny, James, editor. *Sir Gawain and the Green Knight*. Broadview, 1995.

Wojnarowicz, David. *Witnesses: Against Our Vanishing*. Artists Space, 1990.

## Acknowledgments

Small books are hard to write, and this book required an effort that I'm now grateful for — even if, at times, I felt lost within a maze of research. Thanks to my editor, Jen Sookfong Lee, for seeing the potential in my original proposal, and then helping me take it apart so that I could put it back together again. Your feedback, focus, and enthusiasm for the project has been so valuable and most assuredly has made this a better book. Thanks to my students, who I would often ask about Henson-related trivia. They were the initial audience for much of this work, and they gave me the first inkling that *Labyrinth* was a reflection of Henson's mind.

Thanks to Medrie, who often listened to me talk about the perplexity of labyrinths while I worked on this. Thanks, as well, to my partner Devin, who is always willing to fall down a cinematic rabbit hole. I love wandering through life's maze with you. And thanks to Alexis, for reminding me how cool the Muppets are.

Finally, thanks to my parents, for cultivating my sense of amazement. And to Jim Henson, for creating worlds of beautiful monstrosity, compassion, and queer magic.

DEVIL WILGER

**Jes Battis** is a queer autistic writer and teacher, and the author of *The Winter Knight* (longlisted for Canada Reads), *I Hate Parties* (shortlisted for a Lambda Literary Award), the Occult Special Investigator series, and the Parallel Parks series (as Bailey Cunningham). Jes teaches queer and trans studies, medieval literature, and representations of disability/neurodiversity in pop culture at the University of Regina.